# FINANCIAL FIRST AID

# FINANCIAL

# FIRST AID

EMPOWERING PHYSICIANS AND OTHER
PROFESSIONALS TO TAKE CHARGE OF
THEIR FINANCIAL FUTURES

JENNIFER LORD, MD

Library of Congress Control Number: 2017903726
ISBNs: 978-0-9979602-1-1 (paperback); 978-0-9979602-0-4 (hardcover)

Hidden Peak Publishing
Austin, Texas 78703
Printed in the United States of America

Book design by Mayfly Design and typeset in the Chaparrel and URW Grotesk typefaces.

Disclaimer: What is represented in this book is not intended as financial, legal, investment, or accounting advice. The content of this book may not be suitable for everyone and is no way to be construed as advice. Readers should obtain professional advice, as they require. No warranties are made as to the accuracy or completeness of the information presented. The author is not responsible for any liability or loss incurred from the reading or use of this book.

# CONTENTS

# ABOUT THIS BOOK

I decided to write this book because, even after 10–20 years of higher education, most doctors and other professionals that I know have amazingly little financial knowledge.

This book is intended to be a brief overview of personal and business finances. There is a great deal of information not provided in this book. The goal is to provide you with a knowledge scaffold of basic concepts on which you can build further financial knowledge. This basic information will permit you to have educated discussions with financial advisors and experts. In presenting the basics, an attempt has been made to remove the majority of the financial lingo. Some of the terminology used in this book is not what you will hear from the financial industry. For example, when discussing brokerage firms, such companies will be called either "investment houses," which indicates firms that sell their own funds (like Vanguard, Fidelity, and T. Rose Price), or "discount brokerages," which means firms that sell other firms' funds (like online stock brokers). These terms are used here to break these firms down into categories for the reader. I am simply trying to distinguish between those whose funds you may purchase without incurring a transaction fee vs. those that may charge a transaction fee of $6.95 or $9.99 per trade.

Removal of some of the financial lingo is meant to simplify ideas and improve the novice reader's understanding. By simplifying the terminology, in some cases, the terms are not 100% accurate but serve to improve the understanding and comprehension of readers. For example, in the discussion of cost basis in the "Master Limited Partnership" section in chapter 9, "cost basis" is explained as the amount that is "initially invested." However, this is oversimplified, and there are many factors that your accountant will put into the determination of your cost basis. I have chosen to stay out of the weeds and instead aimed to improve reader understanding by simplifying terms rather than to elaborate or to fully represent all terms.

This book provides information for those who would like to invest on their own and save on fees. It also provides basic knowledge to help safeguard you from any unscrupulous financial "professionals" as well as from yourself. There are many ways to invest. Many financial books get bogged down in discussing all possible ways to invest. Such an approach makes it difficult for the novice reader to decide where to begin or what to do next. What is provided here is a way to proceed for those readers who want a starting point. There are many other strategies out there to explore. Keep in mind that a simple strategy usually does better in the long run than a complex strategy that is designed to "beat the market." Usually, boring is best. If you are able to achieve the same returns as the stock market average, you will be better than 95% of the investors out there, including many of the so-called advisors. It's important to understand from the outset that all investing has inherent risks, regardless of what strategy you pursue. You must do your homework and make sure that each investment is suitable to your own situation. If you need help, enlist the assistance of a qualified professional.

This book is designed for professionals, including medical doctors, lawyers, chiropractors, podiatrists, dentists, nurse practitioners, and so on. Many healthcare professionals, including those just mentioned, are called "doctor." For this reason, I may use the term in this book, but I intend for it to refer to all who run their own professional businesses.

# INTRODUCTION

Fifteen Years. That's how long it took after high school. A smart guy graduates at the top of his class in high school. He's idealistic and dreams of helping people by becoming a doctor. He goes to college, plays sports, is president of the student government, and graduates with honors. He takes the MCAT and gets one of the best scores in his college. His whole life has been in preparation for getting into medical school. He goes to medical school, where he graduates with honors. He does a five-year residency training program; works ridiculous hours; and sacrifices time, family, and friends. And then he chooses to do a two-year fellowship in order to specialize in what he really loves. After 15 years of higher education and training, he finally begins private practice $240,000 in debt. He has no savings and no idea how to make a budget or how to run a practice. And he's overwhelmed and afraid to let anyone know that he doesn't know how to do it all.

As students, we spent hours studying, trying to get into professional school. Once we got in, we spent countless years learning our craft. But how much time did we really spend learning about personal and business finances? As professionals, many of us received no training in handling financial matters and yet we are supposed to know how to bill patients and clients, run practices efficiently, and invest wisely in our retirement plans. We may be afraid to ask questions and feel ashamed when we admit that we don't know something. Why are we afraid to ask questions? And who is supposed to teach us?

Why is it that financial education is not deemed as important as acing the MCAT, GMAT, USMLE, boards, or other exams? Why do many medical and professional schools pretend that their professions have nothing to do with money and act like it's a dirty word? It's like parents refusing to have "the talk" with their children about sex, convincing themselves that if they don't talk about it, their children won't be interested in it. It's time for us to at least learn the financial basics so we can protect our families and our futures without blindly taking advice from people whom we presume know more than we do.

There seems to be a belief that people who call themselves financial advisors are more capable of managing our money than we are. Why is that? Is it because they really *are* smarter? Or is it because we are lazy? It's more probable that it's because we lack knowledge and are afraid to admit it, and thus make excuses about why we don't have time to learn it. It is amazing that financial professionals can offer you products and services that you don't understand and that are potentially harmful to your financial future. And no one seems to be held accountable as long as we sign on the dotted line that we understand the risks involved.

Professionals without financial knowledge are easy targets for unscrupulous advisors because of their perceived wealth. And hectic schedules seem to keep us from having the time to research all things financial. We may use the excuse that someone else knows best or that we are too busy to be intimately involved in our financial decisions.

Both our personal finances and our practices can suffer from the lack of knowledge about financial matters. The erroneous belief that the practice is best run by a "manager"—rather than the doctor, lawyer, or other professional who owns it—is somehow accepted and commonplace. We convince ourselves that we are too busy to take on the management and oversight responsibility. I maintain that such a belief is a key reason that many practices suffer mismanagement so easily. It's time to stop letting others direct our financial future. It's time for us to take charge.

As professionals, we have busy lives, and during the few hours of downtime we have at night or on the weekend, we may not feel like reading 15 different financial books in difficult-to-read-and-understand financial lingo. We want to spend it with family and friends or doing our favorite hobbies. This book was designed to quickly cover financial basics that professionals should have learned in all of that schooling but did not. We need to learn it so that we are not taken advantage of by others and do not fall prey to our own ignorance.

What I have realized throughout my life is that even when you are "doing it right," you may still be doing it wrong if you don't understand the basics. When I was a teenager, I started investing in a Roth IRA at the urging of my parents. Despite "doing it right" by investing in the Roth, I still managed to lose a ton of money by blindly listening to my "financial advisor" and investing in her company's mutual funds. By investing in those funds, I wasted 5.5% on a fee for entering into the fund (front-end load), and then wasted another 1% for her to "manage" my money, even though she was doing nothing for me and never met with me again. I had the fund with her for eight years when I decided that I would do a better job managing it myself. When I took over the management, the account value was at the same amount that I had initially invested because of the fees that had been taken out over the years.

Because of these financial experiences and my own lack of financial knowledge, I was on a quest. As I entered college, I decided to get a business degree in addition to the biology degree. I ended up loving the classes so much that I finished with a minor in international business as well. In addition to my class textbooks, I read every financial book I could get my hands on. Then I went to medical school, spent another bunch of years in residency, pursued a fellowship to become a board-certified orthopedic hand and upper extremity surgeon, and went into private practice. Throughout this period I continued to teach myself about finances.

During medical school, I watched students rack up debt. Many had no budgets, and most had credit card debt. Very few had jobs. Almost no one contributed to a Roth IRA. In residency, only a few saved for retirement—most through a 403b and hardly anyone through a Roth. Only a handful paid on their student loans while in training. Interestingly, it wasn't until my third year of orthopedic residency that any financial professionals approached me and my fellow residents about financial planning.

When I started in private practice, all around me were fellow physicians who didn't have budgets, who ran practices without knowing how to read financial statements, and who bought into investments without realizing what they were getting into. I watched some lose a significant portion of their retirement funds in the 2007–2008 recession. Most maximized their 401k/403b contributions and participated in profit sharing while paying down their student loans as fast as possible. But after doing all of that, they ended up buying huge houses, fast cars, and big boats. I vowed that I would not follow in those footsteps but would instead live only slightly "larger" than I had as a resident. I ended up buying a townhome as my first home with the eventual plan of renting it out when I was ready to buy a detached single-family home. My goal was to save money, live well below my means, invest wisely, and be retired before I was 40. I was pragmatic about my investments, and I read every contract in detail. And I was, indeed, retired before I was 40.

I have spent years watching professionals make mistakes. I, too, have made mistakes in this financial rat race. I asked friends of mine who are veterinarians, lawyers, and chiropractors to see if they had received any financial education in school, thinking that it was just medical schools that didn't believe in discussing money. And the majority said no. Just like me, throughout all of the schooling and training, they were never formally taught how to make a budget, plan for retirement, or run a business.

It was then that I realized a huge need for a quick primer on finances. I want to prevent others from making the same mistakes that I have seen or made. The aim of this book is to provide a basic framework on which to build your financial knowledge, to show you the basic "must take care of" items during your career path, and to show you what pitfalls might await you so you can avoid them. And most importantly, I have tried to get rid of most of the financial jargon in order to make the material easier to understand.

The book is broken into four parts. Part I covers what professionals need to address during each stage in their career. Part II covers investment basics, different accounts and when you use each of them, what the different assets are, when to use and how to manage those assets, and what investments you should consider utilizing in different time periods or economic cycles. Part III covers the basics of financial statements, and Part IV covers practice fraud detection and management. The parts of the book cover the knowledge deficits that I have come across most often when talking to other professionals.

Hopefully by the end of this book you will have had an "Aha!" moment and realized that finances are not rocket science or brain surgery. Just remember, getting into medical or graduate school was the hard part, not dealing with your finances.

# PART I

## THE BASICS FOR EACH CAREER STAGE

Many of you are already busy professionals adept at some type of money management. Some of you are just starting out in your career, or maybe even still in school. Wherever you are in your career, the items that I discuss in part I need to be addressed first. Even though some topics may pertain to issues you've handled already in past stages of your career, take a look and make sure you have properly addressed them. These are basic concepts, and even though you may have heard them before, you may have failed to really address and master them.

Do not skip over these items because you believe that you are "beyond" them—that you are too advanced or make too much money to have to deal with these basics. I have yet to find a professional who is so good at budgeting and money management that they never go over that budget. Some of you figure that you will take care of any money issues when you earn a bigger paycheck in the future. Some of you may believe that you make so much money that it doesn't matter if you have a budget or not. It doesn't matter—until it does. You don't want to wake up one day, saying to yourself, "If only I had managed all of that money better, I wouldn't be broke." Or, "I could have retired by now." Even though you may be making a nice paycheck, think of all of those lottery winners out there who won millions only to lose it all in the matter of a few short years. They could have been set for life, but for reasons unknown they never built the foundations of good money management. Now they are back to the grindstone.

# CHAPTER 1

# MEDICAL AND GRADUATE SCHOOL YEARS

Congratulations. You've made it to medical or graduate school. You have worked hard to get here, spent a lot of late nights studying, and made large sacrifices. But after all of that, many of you have neglected what is most important, your financial education. Once you get into medical or graduate school, you figure you've made it to the big time. What students fail to realize is that life does not get easier as it goes on. Many figure that once they start earning a paycheck, finances get significantly less complicated. Ever hear of "more money, more problems"?

The items that I will cover now—budgets, management of student loans, and Roth IRAs—are essential to take care of first. If you haven't already taken care of these things, this chapter will set you on the right road. If you haven't yet dealt with budgeting, managing your student loans, and setting up a Roth IRA, pay close attention to this chapter. It might be boring, but it's vital for you to address these things now. The longer you put off dealing with them, especially the budgeting, the harder it will be for you to get a handle on your finances. People who say that they will "fix things" when they start making more money will never get ahead.

This chapter will look at the following topics:

- Budgeting
- Student Loans
- Roth IRAs

3

# BUDGETING

When I was a student, many of my classmates had no concept of a budget other than that they were able to take out the maximum amount in loans. With that money, they had to pay for tuition, an apartment, books, and food. Beyond that, they just spent whatever they needed, on whatever they wanted, until the money ran out. And then they couldn't wait for the next disbursement. It was really great until they had to pay it all back.

Why does a budget matter? Hopefully, you were lucky enough to apply and get accepted to a state medical school or graduate program. According to 2016 AAMC (Association of American Medical Schools at AAMC.org) data, the cost of attendance for a private medical student was $306,000 for four years, while those who attended a state school paid $232,000. You can end up paying back up to $3 for every $1 you borrow; the less you borrow, the better off you will be, especially if you are attending an expensive private school. You need to develop a budget to help rein in spending. By reining in spending you can ultimately borrow less in loans. And if you never learn to budget when you have little money, it only gets worse when you have tons of money. It is a life skill that no one wants to learn but one that everyone needs to learn.

## HOW TO CREATE A BUDGET

The first step in creating a budget has two parts. The first part is to pull out any bills, invoices, or statements that show how much you spend each month. This step alone can be an eye opener. These include phone bills, rent/mortgage bills, credit card statements, bank statements, and so on. Record everything that you spent money on for the last six months and figure out how much, on average, you spend each month for those items. Even if you are a full-fledged professional, you need to do this step. The second part is determining what your "income" is, even if it is a one-time loan disbursement. To figure out your "income" from your loan, take the loan amount and divide it by the number of months it has to last and then you have your "monthly salary."

Next, make a list of all of the "have to pay" items, like rent/mortgage, electric, tuition, and so on. Then make a list of how much you spend on the variable items, like food. But break that down into "necessary groceries" and "non-necessary food," which includes Starbucks coffee, beer, and take-out food, and so on. Obviously the non-necessary food items do not get listed in the "have to pay" list. Make a gas column, phone, and anything else you spend money on.

Write down your income at the top of a separate piece of paper. Then add entries with the amount of the necessities you will have to spend and sub-tract them from your income. What is left over is called your "disposable income."

Next, add a line for the amount that you are going to *save* each month, including for your Roth IRA if you have a work-study job. Savings be-longs after the necessities. If you wait until you have bought all of the non-essential items, there will be nothing left and you will never save. Savings is a necessity. Some financial experts suggest that savings comes first, even before your necessities. That way you rein in your "have to pay" items as well and you are sure to have contributed to your savings.

Decide what else you really need to spend money on and determine what you can cut out. Put that on the sheet or remove items from the sheet. You still need to have money budgeted for "fun expenses," because you really do need a break from studying, so don't budget all of your fun away. Just rein it in a little if you have a very large "Fun" budget.

Now you have your budget and can tweak it as needed. By creating a bud-get and sticking to it, you will hopefully borrow less in loans than you would have otherwise. Revisit your budget monthly to make sure you are staying on track. You can consider using software like Quicken, a plain old Microsoft Excel spreadsheet, or an app like "Mint" or "You Need A Bud-get," if pen and paper isn't your style. By the way, even if you are no longer a student, you still need to make a budget and stick to it.

By creating a budget, you allot money for what you need and even some for what you want. The budget makes you conscious of what you are spending money on and allows you to consciously decide if you really need what you are buying. If you do not have a budget, there will be much more impulse spending. The goal is to build some discipline in spending and saving.

I know a lot of professionals who do not have discipline when it comes to budgeting, spending, and saving. They are now caught up buying "bigger and better," which is the surest way to the poorhouse. And, it will keep you from reaching the point of financial freedom where you "work because you want to" instead of "because you have to." You have to become disciplined in studying and schoolwork in order to get into medicine, law, or whichever chosen graduate field, so why not carry that over to your finances as well?

## INCLUDING CREDIT CARDS IN YOUR BUDGET

The second step in creating a budget is managing your credit card. I know that most of you have heard this already, but really, it is *that* important. Credit cards can be great if you treat them like cash and buy only if you have the cash available to completely pay off the credit card balance every month. Even so, a study by Dun & Bradstreet revealed that if people use a credit card for purchases, instead of using cash, they will actually spend more overall—even if they have the money in the bank to pay off the credit card each month. If you do happen to have credit card debt and are unable to pay off the balance each month, you need to get that debt under control first.

If you have credit card debt, take that money you would have spent on non-essential items and use it to pay down the debt on the card. You need to pay more than just the minimum balance if you want to get ahead financially. If you say, "Well, I'll just pay it off later when I'm making an attending physician's salary," you might as well pack your bags for the poorhouse.

The average amount of credit card debt per adult with a credit card in the United States in 2016 was $5,280 (from www.Creditcards.com), and the average annualized Percentage Interest Rate (APR) fluctuates but is usually in the high teens or higher. And the credit card companies can compound the interest every day. This means that if you pay only the minimal balance (which is on average 2% of the balance) on $5,280 at 15% APR, it will take you six years to pay off the debt, and you will pay close to $3,000 in interest alone.

Now you may say, "What do I do if I have more than one credit card with debt?" You can choose one of three ways to pay off your cards. The first option is to pay either off the card with the smallest amount of debt or to pick the card with the highest interest rate. Once the first card is paid off, repeat the process for all the other credit cards on which you owe money. Pay down the debt on each card and close the account you just paid off. Doing that can help raise your credit score if you have a lot of open accounts. However, if you close all of your credit cards, it can actually harm your credit score, so keep one or two accounts open. Every time you pay off a card, increase the amount you pay on the rest of the balances, since you have fewer cards to pay on.

You can also contact the credit card company directly and ask for a temporary interest rate reduction to enable you to pay more on the principal, which will enable you to pay off the debt faster. The last resort is to hire a for-profit company to negotiate debt reduction on your behalf. However, you need to make sure that it is a reputable company and know that you may be responsible for taxes on the "forgiven" debt because the IRS sees that as income. The best way to pay off credit card debt is to not create the debt in the first place. One credit card is generally a necessity to own nowadays, but limit it to one or two and shred the offers that come in the mail.

A great resource for credit card debt and budgeting is the National Foundation for Credit Counseling (www.nfcc.org/). If you think that paying off the debt is too hard, just remember that once the cards are paid off, you will have more disposable income since you are not paying all of that interest.

## STUDENT LOANS

"You can take out the maximum amount of loans if you just sign here. You *do* want to take out the maximum loan, right?" That's what the financial aid people asked me. "Uh, I guess so. Where do I sign?"

It's amazing that you can take loans out larger than many people's mortgages without having to be given any really meaningful financial counseling—and with almost no questions asked, either. Once they find out you're starting medical school, law school, a nursing program, or any other graduate program, financial institutions can't wait to start giving you loans. According to AAMC.org (Association of American Medical Colleges), the average debt in 2015 for a graduating medical student was $180,000. And that wasn't figuring in undergraduate debt.

Three main types of educational loans exist: government subsidized loans, government unsubsidized loans, and private loans. The subsidized loans are the better loans to take out, if you can, because the government pays the interest on the loan while you are in school. The unsubsidized loans will begin accruing interest the moment you take out the loans. Obviously, if you can get a grant that doesn't have to be paid back, you would rather have that. And, if at all possible, avoid taking out a private loan. These are unsubsidized and tend to carry higher interest rates; they also may not be eligible for loan consolidation at a later date.

You do not want to take out the maximum amount of loans if you can avoid it. A general rule of thumb is that for every dollar in loans you take out for school, plan on paying up to $3 back. (This depends on how long your schooling is and if you have an indentured servitude you have to do, in addition to school, like residency. The $3 for each borrowed dollar is figuring that you went to four years of school and opted for (1) forbearance during residency or other extra training, and (2) repayment using a 25-year repayment plan.) So that $180,000 can become over $500,000 when you include interest payments. Any way that you can lower the amount that you have to borrow will be a huge savings later on. It's easier to not borrow than to pay back three times as much later.

Adding a work-study job is also very helpful. It not only helps decrease the amount of loans you have to take out but, more importantly, allows you to contribute to a Roth IRA. A Roth IRA is a type of retirement account to which you can contribute only if you are in a lower income tax bracket. And one of the best things you can do for your retirement account is to start it early. Since many doctors and professionals start saving for retirement only after they finish their graduate program and training, you will be far ahead of the curve when it comes to your peers if you start saving while in medical or graduate school instead of waiting until you have a "real job."

## FINANCIAL LITERACY: Compounding

Why care about budgets and loan amounts? They matter because of a principle called compounding. Loans that you take out come with interest charges that you pay for the privilege of borrowing someone else's money. Compounding occurs when you are unable to pay the interest payments and the amount of the interest is then added to the amount of your loan, increasing the principal. The new interest payment is then calculated off of the new principal amount.

For example, if you have a $100,000 loan at 5% interest, your interest payment will be $5,000. If you don't pay it, your principal is now $105,000. The next interest payment is then $5,250. And so on. That is how you can end up paying back $3 in loan repayments for every dollar that you borrow. The higher the interest rate and the more times in a year the loan company compounds the interest, the more you will owe. So if it is compounded every month, you will end up paying more than if it is compounded once a year.

Compounding can also benefit you, like in investing. If you invest in a company or stock, earnings are paid out to you, the stockholder. But instead of being paid out, they can be reinvested to purchase more stock. This increases wealth, because you get earnings on earnings. The main point to understand with compounding is that it is logarithmic. So it doesn't increase at a steady rate. The amount increases very slowly at first, and then—boom!—it begins to take off. The moral of the story is to be patient with investing. You will not double your money overnight. It will probably take 20 years, but then it can really take off.

Notice the curve on the next page.

Now consider the following. You start out with one dollar, and every day the amount doubles from the previous day. So the second day you have $2, the third day there is $4, and so on. How many days until you have over $1,000,000? The answer is 20 days. Yes it's true. However, if you do the math, what you will notice is that during the first 15 days, you will only have accumulated around $32,000. In the

*(continued on next page)*

9

*(continued from previous page)*

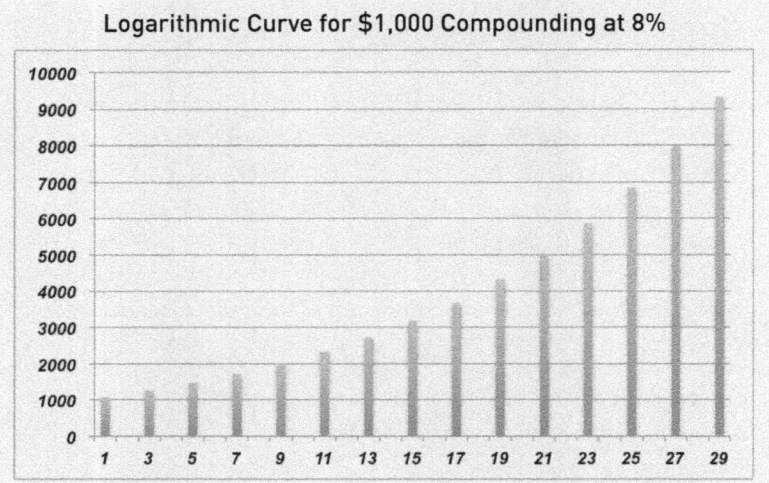

next five days it goes from $32,000 to $1,000,000. So the next time you hear someone tell you to start investing early, you know why. The first 15 years you may not make much headway, but the next bunch of years the account balances can begin to take off.

Just a side note, there is a quick-and-dirty method to figure out how long something will take to double in value. It's called the **Rule of 72**, and it goes like this: If you take 72 and divide it by the interest rate, the resulting number is a rough estimate of how many years it takes for the starting amount to double. For example, if you are making 5% in interest on your investment, then you divide 72/5 = 14.4. So the amount of money will double in a little over 14 years.

## ROTH IRAs

Roth IRAs are important retirement accounts to consider while still a student or still in training as a resident or other indentured servant. "What?" you ask. "Retirement accounts? I'm not even out of school yet and you are talking about retirement accounts?" Yes, for two reasons.

A Roth IRA is a retirement account to which you may contribute only if you are working and only while earning under a certain amount, which may be the case for you only in school, residency, or postgraduate training. This money will grow tax-free (meaning that any gains in account values will not be taxed, even if you buy and sell assets) and is tax-free in retirement. You may only contribute up to the amount of income you have earned for the year, or $5,500 for 2017, whichever is less.

Compounding is the second reason that you want to contribute to a Roth IRA as soon as you possibly can. As discussed earlier, the sooner you invest, the better compounding can work. Any money in this account will be allowed to grow tax-free and will never be taxed again, providing you follow the plan rules. So a small job or work-study in medical school will be more than worth it in the long run.

Consider this. You make a one-time investment of $5,000 when you are 25 years old, compounding at 8% a year, you will have almost $160,000 by retirement at age 65 for doing nothing more than putting $5,000 into a Roth one time. Imagine if you contribute the maximum to a Roth each year ($5,500), starting at age 25, by the time you are 65 you will have contributed $220,000. Assuming it compounds at 8% per year, you will have amassed over $1.6 million. If you start early, compounding does the majority of the work for you.

But if you wait to start contributing until age 45 and contribute the $5,500 each year until retirement at age 65 (20 years of contributing), you will only amass around $310,000. On the flip side, if you start early at age 25 and invest the same $5,500 for the same 20 years and stop contributing at age 45, you will amass over $1.4 million by age 65. So the lesson is to *start early*. If you have any income, you should contribute to a Roth IRA.

Oh, and you don't need to have a financial advisor to set up an account. You can do this yourself. If you feel overwhelmed, don't worry; it's easy to set up this account. You can go online to an investment house like Vanguard or Fidelity and they will help you open the account. (Avoid online stock trading sites because most will have transaction fees). All you have to do is to call them up or go online and tell them what you want to do. If you're worried about which fund is the best to invest in, most experts recommend investing in a fund that is broad based and carries a wide array of stocks, with the lowest fees possible. But I will discuss this more later on. A great type of investment to place your money into is a total stock market fund/ ETF. These tend to have low fees and have broad diversification of stocks. Presumably you will not be close to retirement if you're in school or training and should therefore need minimal bonds in your investment portfolio.

## FINANCIAL LITERACY: Pre- and Post-Tax Money

Now that you have your budget under control, you need to start investing in your retirement account. Because the government wants its tax on your income, you need to determine when you are to pay those taxes. You will utilize different investment tax strategies depending on your investment plan and where you are in your career. You need to understand the difference between pre- and post-tax money. Keep in mind that the government has already predetermined when you pay the tax depending on which account you use. Pre-tax money is used mainly in reference to retirement accounts and health savings accounts. All other investing accounts use post-tax money only.

Using **pre-tax money** means that you invest the money before you pay the tax. This occurs when you contribute to a 401k retirement account, some traditional IRAs, and SEP IRAs. You will not only have a larger amount to invest but the money you contribute to that retirement account will lower your taxable income amount for the year. Because you have not paid tax on the money before you invest it (pretax), you will have to pay tax on it when you withdraw it in retirement.

Using **post-tax money** means that you invest the money after you pay the tax. This occurs in Roth IRAs. The benefit is that any gains that accumulate in the account will not be taxed again when you withdraw the money in retirement and can grow tax-free forever. However, it does not lower your taxable income in the current year.

## TAKEAWAYS

- Roth IRAs are post-tax. That means that the tax is taken out before you invest it. It will grow tax-free in the retirement account and any capital gains will grow unchecked by tax, as well as be tax-free when you withdraw it in retirement. You can only contribute while in a lower tax bracket. Contribute as soon as you can, ideally starting while in school.
- Creating a budget now will help you keep your finances and spending in check and make you aware of what you are buying. This will be invaluable as your paycheck grows.
- Compounding can do the majority of the work for your retirement fund if you begin early.

## TO-DO LIST

- ☐ Create a budget and find out what you spend money on.
- ☐ Pay off credit card debt.
- ☐ Contribute to a Roth IRA if you have an income.
- ☐ Get a work-study job.

# CHAPTER 2

# INDENTURED SERVITUDE YEARS

Hooray! You are finally out of school and ready to start a few years of indentured servitude in your medical residency or other postgraduate training program. Lucky for you it's time to finally start making some money, but now what? What should you do next? This chapter will look at the items you need to address now that you are done with formal schooling and are making a paycheck. The chapter will discuss the following topics:

- Loans Revisited
- Rainy Day Fund
- Disability Insurance
- 401k/403b
- Roth IRA
- Other Considerations

## LOANS REVISITED

Now that you are done accumulating loans, you need to decide how and when to pay them back. You have to decide either to start repaying your loans or to place the loans into deferment/forbearance. The earlier you can begin loan repayment, the less money you will spend on interest in the long run. If you are unable to repay the loans, you can place them into deferment or forbearance, depending on your eligibility for those programs. Consolidation of multiple loans into one loan may make it easier for you to manage your loans and may allow you to lower your interest rate. If you have the money, you should begin to pay on loans while in residency, even if it's a reduced amount. It will significantly decrease the amount you will pay back. And more importantly, it will allow you to take a tax deduction.

For example, you borrowed $100,000 at 5% interest (Perkins loan interest rate) and are now entering a 3-year residency training. Option 1: You decide to pay on your loans. If you pay the loans back over a ten-year period, you will pay over $27,000 in interest in addition to the principle. If you pay back over 25 years, you will pay over $75,000 in interest. Option 2: You choose to forebear the loan during training and then repay over 25 years. In this case, you will end up paying back over $100,000 in interest, more than double what you borrowed.

Regardless of which option you choose, you want to get the best interest rate possible, even a 1% difference can add up to a large sum of money. Sometimes you can consolidate the loans at a better rate. If you pay your monthly payments on time, you may be eligible for a 1%-2% interest rate decrease after paying for a period of 12–36 months. Once you get the rate reduction, remember not to miss any payments. It happened to a friend of mine. He moved between residency and his attending position and changed his bank but forgot to switch the bank for his loans, and he lost his 1% deduction. Over the life of a loan, that can add up. For example, paying 4% instead of 5% for $100,000 over 25 years adds up to a savings of $20,000 in interest just by paying on time and getting a rate reduction.

Finally, there is one last reason to start repaying the loans while in training. Not only can you decrease the amount you will pay in the long run, but by paying during postgraduate training, you can also tax deduct the student loan interest payments. You can deduct up to a maximum of $2,500 each year. However, the student loan tax deduction is only possible while you earn under $80,000 if you are single ($160,000 if married) and is partially phased out starting at $65,000 for singles.

## RAINY DAY FUND

After squaring away how you are going to pay off your loans, you need to establish a rainy day fund. It's a must. It is recommended that you have enough cash on hand to cover six months of living expenses in order to protect yourself in case of illness or emergency. This money is for an emergency and should not be thought of as an investment. And as such, it should be kept in a "liquid" account like a savings account, money market deposit account, or some account that has little risk of losing value. A liquid account simply means that it is easily converted to cash. You could also keep some of this money in a three-month CD (certificate of deposit) provided you have enough cash available for the three months the money is tied up in the CD. This money should not be kept in the stock market or other accounts that may lose value because it may not be there when you need it. Money market deposit accounts can be set up at a bank or online at investment houses like Vanguard or Fidelity (usually they have lower fees than a discount brokerage). CDs and savings accounts can be opened via a bank.

## DISABILITY INSURANCE

Now that you have racked up significant amounts of debt, or even if you haven't, it is extremely important to purchase disability insurance. You have a large earning potential as a professional, and you need to protect that. If anything should happen to you and you couldn't work, the insurance would provide money to pay your loans and living expenses. You would also be able to recoup some of the lost earning potential.

There are two main types of disability insurance to consider, short-term and long-term. If you do not have any money saved in your rainy day fund, you should have a short-term policy that generally covers you for 90–180 days. Once you have enough money in the bank to cover you for those 3–6 months, you can then forgo the short-term disability insurance.

The more important insurance is long-term disability. This should be purchased separate from, or in addition to, any insurance offered by your employer. The coverage provided by your employer is usually less than you will need. And by purchasing your own policy, not only can you get adequate income replacement but you are also assured that you can take the coverage with you if you decide to leave your employer. It doesn't matter so much if you are young and healthy, but once you are mid-career and have a few health issues, you may have a tough time finding affordable insurance if you change jobs and don't have your own policy.

You can pay for disability insurance with pre- or post-tax money. Some people are tempted to save on income taxes by using pre-tax money. Resist that temptation and pay with after-tax dollars. If you use pre-tax money to pay for the insurance policy, any benefits you receive will be taxed before you receive them. So instead of receiving $10,000 for a month you may end up with $7,200 if you are in the 28% tax bracket. That can add up to significantly more money than paying the premiums with post-tax money.

When purchasing disability insurance, you should obtain "own-occupation" insurance if possible. "Own-occupation" means that if you are, say, a surgeon and you are no longer able to operate, the disability insurance will kick in even if you can still see patients in the office. Some of these benefits may last only up to two years, depending on your policy. After that, you may need to be declared completely disabled for benefits to continue. Many of these policies will replace up to 60%–70% of your income, although some can replace as much as 85%. The optional riders will allow you to purchase more income replacement as your income level grows after training without needing a new physical exam. The ideal policy would be an "own-occupation policy" that guarantees benefits to age 65. Be aware that some policies will only provide benefits for two to five years. Make sure you understand how the policy that you purchase works. Ask lots of questions, write down the answers, and keep them with your policy so you'll have them if you need to use the insurance.

In general, the younger you are when you get disability insurance, the cheaper it will be. You will be subjected to a physical exam and blood work. If you develop a disease in the future before you get insurance, the insurance will be more expensive if you can still obtain it at all.

There are some other features that you should look for. Besides "own-occupation," you should get insurance that is "non-cancellable, guaranteed renewable." This means that the policy cannot be canceled for a change in health risk as long as the premium is paid on time, and the policy is automatically renewed every year. The policy rates can be raised but only for all policyholders, not just for one individual, and benefits cannot be decreased or changed by the insurance company.

One note for women: disability insurance rates for women tend to be significantly higher than those for men. Women should consider purchasing disability insurance as part of a group. Then they can get the "unisex" rate, which is usually the same as a "men's" rate. This usually means that there are at least two other people, one of whom is male, buying a policy with you, such as other trainees or practice partners.

You will also need to choose the "waiting period" before the policy starts paying benefits. The longer the waiting period is, the cheaper the premium will be. It can range from 30 days to 180 days. You should have a rainy day fund set aside, so opt for the 180-day waiting period.

I also recommend comparing several insurance companies. The Standard is a very common insurance company choice among doctors. Consider buying straight from the source. If you go through financial advisors, it will make the process easier for you but they may also get a hefty commission from you that you won't even know you are paying. If you do use a financial advisor, make sure you ask how much commission they are receiving by selling you the policy. And again, make sure you know how the policy works, and keep the answers to any questions along with the policy.

## 401k/403b

The 401k and 403b accounts are the retirement accounts generally offered by companies and hospitals. Which one they offer depends on whether they are for-profit (401k) or not-for-profit (403b). Most private practices offer a 401k and most not-for-profit businesses, like hospitals, offer a 403b. Starting as soon as possible, you need to contribute the maximum to these retirement accounts. The reasons are, as stated earlier, tax deductions and compounding. The later you start to contribute to your retirement, the less your money will make through compounding and the more you need to make up through contributions. The other factor is that if you contribute to the 401k/403b, the amount that you contribute will lower the amount of income that you will be taxed on that year. So if you are in training, making $50,000, and you contribute $10,000 to your 401k, you will only pay tax on $40,000.

This money will grow tax-deferred for the next 40 years. That means you don't pay taxes on the gains until you withdraw the money, allowing compounding to work that much harder for you. Some employers also have an employee "matching" program, which means that for every dollar you contribute to your account, your employer will contribute one dollar to your account, up to a certain amount (usually 3%-6% of your salary). This is free money that you will miss out on if you do not contribute.

## ROTH IRA

You should also contribute the maximum to a Roth IRA. This is important because your residency/training years may be the last time you are allowed to contribute to a Roth IRA. For 2017, you may contribute up to $5,500/year, and the contributions stop once you reach $133,000 adjusted gross income filing as a single person and $196,000 filing jointly. You can contribute to this along with the 401k/403b.

## OTHER CONSIDERATIONS

Once professionals have squared away their loans and they're making a paycheck, the tendency is to want to upgrade. They want to move out of their apartments and abandon their beaters for home ownership and a fancy new car. But here are a few things to consider before doing so.

### HOMES

Buying a home is a great idea once you have income to afford a mortgage. If you do not have money for a down payment, you probably should not be buying a house yet. You should understand that if you want to retire early or only "work because you want to," you should not buy the largest house around. I bought a town home that I planned on renting out as an income property once I had saved enough money to afford a slightly larger home. It did not bother me that other physicians were living in mansions on golf courses or on the lake with private boat docks.

You can take a tax deduction for the mortgage interest on your home for a mortgage of up to $1,000,000 (if married and filing separately, the limit is $500,000). You should know that when taking out a mortgage on a primary residence you will have to pay PMI (private mortgage insurance) unless you have put a 20% down payment or you have paid 20% of the mortgage off. This is a wasted fee. It does nothing for you. If you have the 20% to put for your down payment, you probably should do so unless you have investment opportunities with significantly better returns. And in general, it is recommended that you take out the loan for the longest time period possible. "What?" you ask. You may have heard from other financial experts that you want to pay off your home as quickly as possible. Yes, this can be true, but only if you are *not* disciplined.

If you *are* disciplined, it is a better idea to take as long as possible to pay off your mortgage. "Why?" you ask. When you take out a mortgage, in the beginning, the payments are made up of mostly interest and include only a little of the principal. The longer the repayment period, the higher the percentage of interest is in the monthly payment. Why would I want to pay more in interest? Thanks to the IRS, you are allowed to deduct your primary residency's mortgage interest from your income. This is one of the few deductions allowed when you make over a certain income level. So the longer the mortgage, the larger the interest portion will be that you can deduct from your taxable income and possibly lower your income level to a lower tax rate.

Now comes the disciplined part. The longer you can stretch out your mortgage payments, the lower your monthly payment will be. If you are disciplined and take the difference from what you are paying on a 30-year mortgage compared to what you would have paid on the 15-year mortgage, or that extra mortgage payment you were going to make to pay down the mortgage faster and put it into an investment account, you will have significantly more money than if you paid off your mortgage. How is that possible?

Let's look at Doctor A and Doctor B, who both take out $250,000 mortgages. Doctor A has taken his mortgage out over 15 years at 3.5% APR because he wants to pay it off ASAP. His monthly payment is around $1,800. Doctor B has a 30-year mortgage at 4% APR. Her monthly payment is around $1,200. The difference in the amounts from what Doctor A is paying and what Doctor B is paying is $600/month. Doctor B invests this $600, for example, in a Vanguard total stock market index fund (averaging slightly over 9% per year since inception, according to Vanguard). At the end of 15 years, she has $232,000 in her investment account and $160,000 left on her mortgage.

At the end of 15 years, Doctor A has now paid off his mortgage. He is still working full time, but is no longer able to take advantage of the mortgage interest deduction on his taxes. Meanwhile, Doctor B continues taking mortgage interest deductions, and she continues to invest the $232,000 in the investment account. If she needed to, she could pay off her mortgage and still have $72,000 left over. As you can see, Doctor B will make out far better than Doctor A.

So if you are disciplined and invest the money instead of spending it, it is far wiser to take a longer mortgage at a higher interest rate with a lower monthly payment and invest the difference. However, if you are not disciplined and spend every last penny, then by all means, pay off your mortgage as quickly as possible. Or if you are planning to retire soon and will not need the mortgage deduction, pay off the mortgage. You still want to take out the mortgage for as long a time period as possible, but make sure there is no pre-payment penalty. That way you still have the option to pay it off quickly or take the mortgage deductions if you decide to become disciplined or decide not to retire.

There is one further comment on home purchases. If you sell your primary residence for a gain, you are able to make a profit of $250,000 for singles, or $500,000 if married, over what you initially paid for it without being taxed on the capital gains. However, you have to meet two criteria, which seem a bit redundant. The first is that in a five-year period, you must have owned the home for at least two of the five years. And second, in a five-year period, you must have lived in the home for at least two of the five years in order to qualify for the deduction. Check the IRS website for all of the rules.

## CARS

Once you have a job, the next inclination is usually to buy or lease a new car. After I had graduated from my residency training program, a family member gave me a free Pontiac Grand Prix beater. It had 170,000 miles on it, the power windows didn't work, and I ran it into the ground until the power steering went out. It was *awesome* because there was *no* car payment.

According to Edmunds Inc., a new car loses 10% of its value once you drive it off the lot. And a car can lose up to 20%–40% of its value the first year, depending on the car type. The smartest way to obtain a car is to purchase it outright and keep it as long as possible. If you are able, use cash and avoid the car loan unless it is 0% APR. You are better off purchasing a car that is one or two years old. If you lease a car, get ready to throw money away, especially if you are a terrible negotiator. The dealers can trick you into a lease with lots of hidden fees. A car is not an investment; it does not make you money. Its only purpose is to get you from point A to point B, and any extra fees or lease payments will make it that much longer for you to work "because you have to" rather than "because you want to." If you must buy an expensive sports car, remember that the purchase is not an investment but a very large fun expense that you need to factor into your budget.

## FINANCIAL LITERACY: Creating Your Personal Financial Statement

When creating your personal financial statement (PFS), you need to understand assets and liabilities. **Assets** are things that are owned by a person or company. Cash, furniture, cars, and jewelry are assets. They have a monetary value. Non-tangible items like patents are also considered assets. **Liabilities** are debts or financial obligations. These include your car loan, rent (if you signed a lease) or mortgage, student loans, and credit card debt.

You need to take your financial picture now and make a plan of where you want to be in one, five, and ten years. Then make a road map to get you to your destination. For example, your destination may be that you want to be credit card debt-free in six months, pay

*(continued on next page)*

(continued from previous page)

off your student loans in four years, be retired by age 40, or even all three. You can't get somewhere specific in a timely fashion if you don't know where you are going or how you are going to get there.

You need to decide what you must do to get you to where you want to go. You need to look at your PFS every quarter, semi-annually, or annually to see if you are headed in the right direction to achieve your goals. By checking frequently, you can correct your course before you get too far off the path. If you don't check frequently, you can get so far off course that you may not be able to get back on the path you wanted to be on.

You should start creating your PFS with a list of your assets and liabilities and the amount of each. Some of you will have minimal assets, maybe a savings or checking account, and several liabilities. That is okay, as long as you have a plan and take action on that plan. For example, when I started residency I had the assets and liabilities shown in the following table.

| ASSETS | | LIABILITIES | |
|---|---|---|---|
| Car | | Credit card debt | |
| Furniture | | Student debt (college/graduate) | |
| Roth IRA | | Rent (signed lease) | |
| Savings & Checking | | Car loan | |

My initial goal was to pay off my credit card debt. I designed a budget that would allow me to keep extra money held back to pay off that debt. I revisited my PFS and budget quarterly and made sure that I was doing what I said I was going to do. After I paid off my credit card debt, I went after the car loan until it was paid off. The next goal was to begin saving. Since I had fewer expenses going out every month, it was much easier to save money now that I was no longer paying on the car and the credit card. But had I not revisited my financial statement and budget, I may not have realized that I was beginning to spend more on fun and less toward paying off the credit card debt and the car loan.

It is okay to have a negative net worth in the beginning. The purpose of making the PFS is to know where you are and decide where you want to go.

A PFS looks like the following.

## PERSONAL FINANCIAL STATEMENT FOR DR. X

| ASSETS | | LIABILITIES | |
|---|---|---|---|
| Cash (checking and savings) | $400 | Car Loan | $4,200 |
| Personal Property | $2,800 | Student Loan | $43,000 |
| Car | $8,000 | Rent (for12mths) | $6,000 |
| Roth IRA | $1,500 | Credit Card | $2,300 |
| TOTAL ASSETS | $12,700 | TOTAL LIABILITIES | $55,500 |

**NET WORTH (Total Assets –Total Liabilities)**          **($42,800)**

**TAKEAWAYS**

- Disability long-term insurance: Look for an own-occupation policy, with six- month waiting period that is non-cancellable, and guaranteed renewable. Consider additional income riders. If you are a woman, try to get a group rate.
- Assets are things you own; liabilities are things you owe.
- Cars lose significant value once you take them off the lot. Avoid leases and consider buying a car that's one or two years old.
- Postgraduate training may be the last time you can contribute to a Roth IRA.

**TO-DO LIST**

☐ Consider student loan consolidation and defer them or set up a payment plan. Be careful not to miss any payments that will increase your interest rate. If you can afford to pay even a little on them, do so.

☐ Purchase long-term disability insurance.

☐ Start saving a rainy day fund, usually six months of expenses.

☐ Contribute the maximum to your 401k/403b.

☐ Contribute to a Roth IRA.

☐ Don't forget to take a tax deduction for student loan interest (up to $2,500) if you are paying on your loans and meet the income requirements.

☐ Create your Personal Financial Statement and update once a year at a minimum.

# CHAPTER 3

# PRACTICE YEARS

Many doctors and professionals will become high-income earners and will wonder, "Now what? I have finally arrived, but do I buy a car or a new home? Or do I invest in the stock market or real estate?" Many get thrown into earning power without really having a plan on what to do with all of the newly earned money. Some feel entitled to buy expensive things after having been deprived for so many years. There are plenty of advisors who are more than happy to help the uninformed professional "invest" their money. Unfortunately, a significant number of doctors and professionals learn about investing the hard way, through trial and error. A little knowledge may help keep you out of harm's way. There are still a few more basics you need to address before deciding what to spend your money on.

This chapter will look at the following topics:

- Disability Insurance
- Life Insurance
- Contributing to Your Retirement Plan
- Other IRAs
- Financial Planners: What You Should Know

## DISABILITY INSURANCE

The first thing you need to do, if you do not already have it, is to get disability insurance—immediately. If you are injured, your entire lifetime earning potential may go down the drain, unless you have a policy; not to mention, being unable to pay the medical debt and student loans. As stated in the last section, the best long-term disability insurance is own-occupation that is non-cancellable and guaranteed renewable. Most insurance companies will allow you to get insurance benefits that reimburse up to 60%–70% of your income and can last for either two years or until age 65 depending on your policy. It goes without saying that you want the policy that lasts until you are 65. If you are already independently wealthy from a prior non-medical career, have no loans and no dependents, you may not need this insurance. Do not buy things that you do not need.

## LIFE INSURANCE

Life insurance is important to have if you have financial obligations or a family to support. The life insurance can protect your dependents financially if you die and have little money saved. The purpose of life insurance is to protect your family's present living standard and to take care of financial obligations. You need life insurance if you have young children whose college you are responsible for paying, are caring for an elderly parent, or have a mortgage and other financial responsibilities. If you are 63 years old with no debt, all of your children are grown, and you have no financial responsibilities, you won't need life insurance. So make sure you crunch the numbers to determine if you need it and how much you really need.

How much do you need? You will first need to estimate how much money your family members use each year to maintain their present living standards and factor in any debt that you owe. Next, you need to figure a conservative estimate on the rate of return that you would earn on the investment of the life insurance benefits that your family would receive (4%–5% per year is a fairly conservative number). You then take that number (rate of investment return) and divide it into the amount that your family needs and the amount of the debt you pay each year. The quotient is the amount of term life insurance that you need in order to maintain your family's current standard of living.

For example, let's say your family spends $50,000 a year (this includes payment on the $500,000 debt you owe for student loans and mortgage, etc.). Let's hypothesize that your family will earn a return on the money invested from the life insurance policy of 4% per year. In this case, you will need $1,250,000 of life insurance for your family to have $50,000/year provided by the investment returns ($50,000 ÷ .04 = $1,250,000). That is assuming that your investments are making a 4% return per year. If your money is not making that rate of return, you may only have enough money to last for 25 years ($1,250,000 ÷ $50,000 = 25).

If you have a significant amount saved already, you may need less in insurance. If you have young children who will need college tuition paid in 15 years, or other large looming future expenses, you may need more. Do not include your retirement accounts in the amount that you have saved. These will need to be used in retirement and cannot be used for current living expenses.

There are two main classifications, the **term policy** (term life) and the **permanent policy**. A term policy is one that is in place *only* for a set period of time. After the term has expired, there is no residual value and the policy is worthless. A permanent policy is one that is in place without a time limit unless you cancel the policy or cash it in, death benefits are paid out, or you forget to pay the premiums. It is *permanently* in place. Permanent policies include whole life, universal life, and variable life policies, all of which are typically used for estate planning purposes rather than for the death benefit—although with the current estate tax laws they are no longer used as frequently.

One other point is that it is better to obtain your own life insurance policy instead of purchasing the one at work. There are two reasons for this. The first is that the term life offered at work is usually more expensive than one you could get individually, since the likelihood of someone dying in your workplace is greater due to the increased number of people in the insurance pool, than the risk that you alone will die. The second is that if you leave your company, you will not be able to take the policy with you, and you might not be able to get a reasonably priced policy later on if you do need to get one yourself.

## TERM LIFE POLICY

Term life is a policy with a term—a limited number of years you can have the policy. Terms may be five, ten, 20, or even 30 years, and the premiums may increase or the benefits decrease as you age. Although you can purchase a policy that has a level premium and benefit for a certain number of years, it may change after that period is over. If you do not pass away before the term is up, there is no residual value to the policy. This type of policy is great if you need some protection for a finite period of time. For example, if you are financially responsible for children until they are finished with college, or for a sick parent for whom you are caring, a term life policy would be desirable. There is no investment component, and if you do not pay the premium on time, the policy is canceled. These are the least expensive policies. A term policy will only be needed until you have amassed enough savings to allow you to "self-insure." Once you reach that point, you can get rid of the expense of term life insurance. If you reach a point in life where you have limited financial responsibilities, you should also get rid of the policy.

## PERMANENT POLICIES

Permanent policies are typically used more for estate planning purposes than for the death benefit, although with the current estate tax laws they are no longer used as frequently. These are much more expensive than term policies because they do not have an expiration date. Usually it is wise to avoid permanent policies unless you and your tax planner have specific reasons to utilize them. But I will discuss them here in case you are advised to use one of these policies. Bear in mind that these policies may generate large commissions for the person selling you the policy and tend to have very high fees associated with them.

### WHOLE LIFE

A whole life policy is a permanent policy that has two components. One is the death benefit (or face value), and the other is an investment component (or cash value) that accumulates over time. The premiums are more expensive than term life insurance due to costs and commissions, but generally the premiums remain level throughout your life. The insurance company takes the investment component of the premium and invests it. In doing so, they guarantee a certain increase in cash value per year until the policy is surrendered or cashed in. But it takes several years before there is an actual cash value. You can borrow against the cash value if needed. It's tax-free but must be paid back with interest or it will reduce the cash value or the death benefit if not paid back. And unlike the term life policy, the death benefit is not limited to a certain length of time. Withdrawals of the cash value are tax-free up to the amount invested. Some policies may even have dividends, which are seen as a return of your money invested in the policy and not taxed. The downside is that these policies have surrender periods of five to ten years before you can take the cash value and cancel or surrender the policy without facing stiff penalties. If you are inclined to get a permanent policy, then whole life is usually your safest option. But a whole life policy should generally not be in lieu of a term policy. It's just too expensive.

## UNIVERSAL LIFE

This permanent policy has premiums that are adjustable if your financial picture or needs change. This policy allows you to decrease or increase your premiums, and consequently your benefits, as needed. The investment component is also tied to mutual funds; as such, the rate of return for the cash value is not guaranteed. This can be especially risky in times of low interest rates. Since the rate of return is not guaranteed, you may have premiums that increase drastically as you age to cover the cost of the insurance, as the investment part may not be doing well enough to help keep the payments down.

## VARIABLE LIFE

A variable life policy is a permanent policy with a guaranteed death benefit, and like the universal policy, the premiums and benefits are adjustable. The difference between the universal life and variable life is that the variable life policy allows the cash value part to be invested in different investment vehicles instead of only mutual funds, making it even more risky than the universal life; and there is no guaranteed rate of return. These policies are classified as securities, and like stocks, have inherent investment risks. These should be avoided. There are better options for investments out there with less risk and much lower commissions and fees.

## WHICH ONE DO I WANT?

Usually term life is the best and cheapest option if your intent is to protect your family's present standard of living. Some financial professionals will try to sell you the permanent policies as excellent investment vehicles or as estate planning tools. But for 2017, estates less than $5.49 million per person have no use for such a tax-planning tool, as there are tax exemptions in place from the government for estates less than that amount. And as far as being considered as an investment vehicle, yes, in addition to providing the standard life insurance, the money grows tax deferred. However, these policies generally come with large fees and expenses. Do the math. It's probable that a run-of-the-mill total stock market fund is a much better option as an investment. And don't forget that the prevailing interest rate will have an effect on how well the life insurance policy serves as an investment vehicle.

If your financial planner is pushing a permanent life policy, ask if he or she is serving you under the fiduciary standard, which means that the financial planner has your financial interest at the forefront of their decision-making. See "FINANCIAL PLANNERS: WHAT YOU SHOULD KNOW," later in this chapter. If not, they may be pushing the policy for a large commission for themselves. And, they can keep getting those commissions for the life of your policy. Life insurance can be a tax-planning strategy, so check with your tax attorney. Be wary and ask questions. Do not buy anything you do not completely understand. And write down the answers to your questions so if you want to know about your policy ten years from now, you still have the answers to your questions.

## OTHER LIFE INSURANCE POLICIES

**Convertible term** is a type of insurance that is initially a term policy, but has slightly higher premiums and can be converted to a permanent policy if needed without new underwriting and physical exams. **Annual renewable** policies are policies that can be renewed each year without a new physical exam, but the premiums will increase each year.

# CONTRIBUTING TO YOUR RETIREMENT PLAN

At this point, you may be excluded from deducting student loan interest from your income tax, or from contributing to a Roth IRA because your income level is too high. So you want to contribute the maximum amount to your retirement plan. This will help shield some of your income from taxation (see "TAX MATTERS" in chapter 4 for more information).

Busy professionals usually tell me that they do not have time to figure out what they should invest in and randomly pick a few mutual funds, one of each fund type offered in their retirement plan, or the fund that had the highest return last year. These methods are generally terrible ways to pick investments. A 401k or 403b retirement plan at work typically has limited choices. Your best bet, if it's offered, is a broad based index fund like a total stock market fund from a company like Vanguard or Fidelity, as they tend to have very low fees and hold very diverse stocks. These, however, may not be offered. Another great fund for the busy, hands-off professional is a target date fund.

Target date funds usually are well diversified and are adjusted according to the time remaining until your retirement date. They carry a mix of stock and bond offerings that correspond to how far away you are from retirement. As your retirement date nears, the fund automatically switches you into more bonds and fewer stocks. If you pick a target date fund, you do *not* pick other mutual funds also. All of your money goes into the target date fund. If you also invest in other mutual funds, this will ruin the diversification provided by picking the target date fund. See "TARGET DATE FUNDS" in chapter 5 for help on choosing the best target date fund.

If neither the total stock market fund nor target date fund is available, you will need to choose a few mutual funds. If there are many mutual funds offered, start by looking for those with the lowest fees. Look at the front page of the fund prospectus to see what the fund's fees are. You can also easily find this online. Look for the "total expense ratio." You are looking for funds with very low fees. Ideally you want funds with less than 0.5% fees. If there are funds with high fees, you should immediately exclude those, because they will eat away at any profits. I don't care how well they have performed in the past. If you see high fees, automatically cross them off your list. (See "KEEPING COSTS LOW" in chapter 6 for more explanation).

Next, you should get a representative sampling of these funds to diversify your portfolio. For example, you may want to pick a stock fund that is a "large cap", one that is a "small cap", as well as a "growth" and a "value" fund. The stock fund type may be listed as part of the fund's name, like Vanguard's "US Growth" fund, or in the prospectus, which is available online. (See "STOCKS" in chapter 9 for an explanation of the different stock types). You may also want to get a small amount of an international fund. Do *not* look at the historical returns and base your fund picks on the funds that have the largest historical returns. Usually the ones that had the highest returns over the last few years will then become some of the worst performing. Low fees and diversification are your top priorities. You could also ask your retirement plan administrators if they could add a total stock market fund or target date fund with low fees. Sometimes they will be able to accommodate you. And you would be doing a favor for all involved in the 401k/403b at your work.

If you have more than five years to retirement, it is generally recommended that you should be mostly in stocks rather than bonds. It's important that you invest in *something*. Having your money in a money market account does not help get you toward your retirement goal. It will only take you an hour or two, and even though it may seem overwhelming, give it a try based on the recommendations above. It will be a lot easier than it first seemed.

If for any reason you leave your practice, consider rolling over your 401k to an IRA. If you do so, *do not* have them send you a check. It should be directly rolled over to another appropriate investment institution into an IRA to avoid stiff penalties from the IRS. You can do this easily through an investment house like Vanguard or Fidelity, where they will help you do the rollover. Your financial planner could also do this for you, if you have one. Before doing a rollover, make sure to check your state's laws regarding which retirement accounts are protected from creditors. It may make sense to leave it in a 401k depending on your situation. I will discuss this further in "401k/403b" in chapter 5.

## OTHER IRAs

It may be that your income level will be too high to contribute to a traditional IRA and get any tax benefit. If you will not get a tax benefit with a traditional IRA, it is generally recommended that you do not contribute to it because of tax and paperwork issues, although it depends on your individual situation. So check with your financial team to see what is best for you. See "TRADITIONAL IRA" in chapter 5.

If you are self-employed, you may be eligible to contribute to a Solo 401k or a SEP IRA. These will usually only work for those physicians doing locum tenens or professionals who are in a consultation business where they are the only employee. See "SEP IRA/Solo 401k" in chapter 5 for more information on these two types of IRAs.

## FINANCIAL PLANNERS: WHAT YOU SHOULD KNOW

There are many types of financial planners with all sorts of letter designations after their names. The only ones you want to work with are those that work under the **fiduciary standard**. This means that the advisor has a fiduciary responsibility to you; he or she must put your financial needs first when making recommendations to you. (There is almost no correlation to the letter designations after their names as to whether or not they have fiduciary responsibility to you.) Some financial planners work under the **suitability standard**, which means that those advisors can only recommend those investments that are suited to your situation and risk tolerance, but this does not mean that they have to put your best interest above their own. Other financial planners are those who do not meet any type of standard. They make money off of products they sell you, without keeping your interests at the forefront, like some brokers. Brokers are commission-based and usually have to sell the funds or products that their company or bank offers. They can have a conflict of interest when it comes to serving you in a fiduciary capacity because they must generally sell their company's funds and offerings instead of offering what is best for you.

There are many different letter designations you will see. Most of these designations refer to a particular exam that they passed or particular types and duration of education and training that they have taken. I'll only cover a few letter designations, as all of this can get very confusing. There are RIAs, which are Registered Investment Advisors who have taken certain "Series" exams and met certain requirements. ("Series" exams are the different financial exams advisors may take. There are Series 3, 5, 6, 7, 11 exams, which test different subjects. The most common is the Series 7 exam, which tests general securities knowledge for stockbrokers.) These advisors are held to a fiduciary responsibility. However, here is where it can get confusing. Advisors are not allowed to use an RIA designation after their name. It is really attached to the firm where they are working. And unscrupulous advisors may try and trick you by attaching an "IAR" (Investment Advisor Representative) after their name to confuse you. An IAR has no fiduciary responsibility and must sell his or her companies' products. Then there are CFPs (Certified Financial Planners), who have education that covers the field of financial planning and are required to maintain their certification. They are a bit like a family medicine practitioner. They are well versed in budgeting, insurance products, retirement accounts, and so on. They may or may not have fiduciary responsibility, so you need to find out how they are paid and if they have fiduciary responsibility. There are also CFA (Certified Financial Analysts), who claim they are the highest level of certification. However, depending on what other designations they have, they may be more adept at managing your stock portfolio than creating an all-around financial plan if they are not also a CFP. Don't get caught up in the alphabet soup that is financial planning designations. What you need to make sure of is that whoever you choose has fiduciary responsibility to you.

How do financial planners get paid? Fee-based financial planners charge you a flat fee for creating an investment plan for you, or they may charge for the time spent advising you. They will typically have your best interests in mind because they do not earn a living by selling you something you do not need. Just because they are fee-based does not always mean that they have fiduciary responsibility to you—you must always ask. Others financial planners earn a living by selling you products and collecting paid commissions from the companies whose products they sell or the funds they invest you in. Some of those commissions may continue to be paid to the advisor for as long as you hold the product, like some insurance policies. Advisors can also be paid with a combination of fees and commissions, such as a wrap fee, which they charge you for managing your portfolio and perhaps take 1% of the money you have invested with them, also known as "asset value under management," each year to do so. The best option is probably a fee-based planner with fiduciary responsibility who creates a plan for you and your particular situation, as they usually have no incentive to sell you something you do not need. They can manage that plan for you, too, for a fee, if you need help.

You should probably stay clear of "investment advisors" found at your local banks. These advisors usually must sell you their companies' products and do not have any fiduciary responsibility to you. If they do have "fiduciary responsibility" to you, then you can consider using them, but be wary.

When choosing a financial planner, you should meet with several to get a feel for them and their staff. Do they seem responsive to you and do they bother asking what your goals are? Be aware of those who are simply interested in how much money you have to invest. Those who ask about your life situation, whether you have children or elderly parents that you are responsible for, your future financial needs among other things, tend to be looking at your whole picture and will create a plan accordingly.

Items to ask a potential financial planner include:

1. Do they have a fiduciary responsibility to you? If not, look elsewhere.
2. Have they ever been convicted of criminal activity or been a subject of financial investigation?
3. What are their fees? How do they get paid, and who pays them?
4. What, specifically, are the financial planner's credentials? Verify them by doing your own research.
5. What services does their firm offer? What type of clients do they specialize in? You want a firm that offers services you need (like insurance, estate planning, etc.).
6. What type of investments do they use? Do they gravitate toward low-fee funds, or do they recommend constant stock trading and use derivatives? Make sure the investment types match your comfort zone. If you see they invest in products

from insurance companies, beware. If you see investments in funds from Vanguard, Fidelity, and other low-cost investment companies, you are probably okay.

7. How often do they meet clients? Is it only once a year? Or do they check in quarterly? And are you working with only one person, or is there a whole team? Who sets up the meeting? The client or the planner? How many new clients do they take on each year? The lower the number, the more personalized care.

8. Do they own the same products and investments that they are going to sell you?

9. Ask them how they handled their clients in 2008 at the recession. Did they hold steady, or did they recommend selling all of their clients' stocks?

10. Ask them about why they lost the last client they lost and why they let the last client go. That will provide insight into how they handle clients.

If you don't like their fees, or how they invest for clients, don't buy their services. There are plenty of good planners out there. Just because someone says that "they are the best in town" doesn't mean that they will be the best for you. And if you have a financial planner now and don't like how they are managing your money or the fees they are taking, talk to them. If they won't make a change, then move your money to someone who will listen to you. You can look up www.napfa.org/ or www.feeonlynetwork.com/ to find fee only financial planners, or www.cfp.net if you need help finding a CFP.

Also recommended is getting a tax advisor, whether that is a tax attorney or CPA who specializes in tax planning, who can help you to decide how to best handle your particular tax situation. They are indispensable and will more than earn their keep. I would get tax advisors early so you can minimize the impact of taxes on your earnings.

## TAKEAWAYS

- Life insurance comes as "term," which last for only a specific period of time, or "permanent," which is in place unless unpaid or canceled. Term policies are the least expensive and good to protect your family until you have accumulated savings. Permanent policies can be expensive, but depending on your situation, may be good for estate planning or investment purposes. These usually are associated with large commissions.
- Financial planners should have fiduciary responsibility to you.

## TO-DO LIST

☐ Get disability insurance if you have not already. The type you want is *own-occupation*, *non-cancellable*, *guaranteed renewable*.

☐ Get term life to cover your earning potential and bills, and possibly whole life if needed for your situation.

☐ Fill up your rainy day fund if you have not already done so.

☐ Contribute the maximum to your retirement plan at work and really sit down and look at the funds offered. Don't just pick them at random or based off of historical returns; go for those with the widest array of stocks and the lowest fees.

☐ Continue to make on-time student loan payments.

☐ Get a financial planner, if needed. Make sure he or she is *fiduciarily responsible* to you.

☐ Get a tax advisor and/or a CPA.

☐ If you leave a practice, consider a rollover of your work's retirement plan to an IRA. See the section "401k/403b" in chapter 5, which discusses rollovers and why and how to do them.

# PART II

## INVESTING FOR PROFESSIONALS

It seems as if there are infinite possibilities for investment choices. Everywhere you turn you find investment advice—books, TV, newspapers, radio, Internet, friends, family, and even the guy at the coffee shop. So why do experts recommend certain investments over others? It never seems as if there is a rhyme or a reason for their suggestions. Despite the seemingly random process, there are some ground rules to keep in mind that may make the process of investing easier and more scientific than it first seems. And it doesn't require you to learn how to read stock chart trends or dig up past performance statistics. Part II will cover the amount you need to save for retirement, explain investing basics, guide you through why you invest in what, and teach you how to evaluate your different investment choices.

# CHAPTER 4

# WHAT YOU NEED TO KNOW FOR RETIREMENT

You're ready to start saving for retirement. But where do you start? This chapter will cover the following to help you make a road map to get you to your retirement destination.

- Know Your Number
- Tax Matters
- Portfolio Diversification

## KNOW YOUR NUMBER

The most important place to begin is to know where you want to end up. And the first thing you need to know is "your number." Your number is the amount of money that you will need to accumulate by retirement, so that you can live as you want to in retirement. So how do you get that number?

You need to determine the level of income you will need per year in retirement. Most experts recommend 80% of your current income, although depending on where you are in your career, this percentage may vary widely. It is important to revisit this number to make sure you are on track to achieve your goals.

Why 80%? Why not your current income? Generally, you will pay less tax in retirement because you will usually fall into a lower income tax bracket than during practice and will not have to pay FICA tax, and you will no longer be paying contributions to your 401k and other retirement accounts. However, if you plan on a significant amount of traveling or leading a more extravagant lifestyle in retirement than you currently lead, you may need to increase your number.

Now to determine **the amount you need to accumulate by retirement**, take the amount you need per year and divide it by 4% (or .04). This is your number. It may seem excessively large if you have not calculated this number before. Why did I divide it by .04? Most experts agree that you can withdraw up to 4% per year without depleting your retirement funds over the span of your retirement. (Although the new prevailing thought is that you may need to plan for 2%–3% returns considering the low interest rate environment we have been in lately.) If you plan on having nothing left for heirs when you die, then you may be able to withdraw more.

CURRENT SALARY × .80 = $ _____

$ _____ ÷ .04 = YOUR NUMBER

You do not have to save all of this yourself. You will probably be eligible for Social Security income unless Congress changes the law in the future. Even so, this will most likely be a very small percentage of what you need.

Now, you need to determine how much you will expect to receive from Social Security at retirement. As of 2017, you will not get full benefits unless you start taking disbursements after age 66, with an increase in benefits the longer you defer taking it. If you collect Social Security at age 62, your benefits could be reduced by 32% or more. This is a very difficult number to calculate exactly. It is easier to look at your statements, which usually come once a year. On the statement you can find the amount you can expect to receive in retirement. You can also go to the following website to find out your amount: www.ssa.gov/retire/. Subtract this number from your 80% of current income number and divide that number by .04. This will give you the amount that you need to save.

## TAX MATTERS

Before considering how best to start accumulating retirement funds, you need to understand the impact that taxes can have. Most professionals will presumably be in a higher tax bracket during their career than in retirement; when you are a student or an indentured servant, of course, you will be in a lower bracket. So different investment strategies are utilized at different times to try to shelter your money from as much tax as is legally possible. I strongly recommend getting a tax attorney and a CPA as part of your team of advisors so they can determine where you can get the most tax relief for your situation.

When discussing investing, there are two types of money and two types of accounts that you need to understand. There are **pre-tax** and **post-tax money**, and there are **tax-advantaged accounts** and **tax-disadvantaged accounts**. As I have previously discussed, pre-tax and post-tax money simply refer to when you pay the tax on the money that you are investing. The pre-tax money and post-tax money terminology is used in reference to your retirement accounts or the tax-advantaged accounts. Tax-advantaged and tax-disadvantaged refer to whether or not the government allows tax breaks on the capital gains or dividends that occur inside the account.

If you are using **pre-tax money**, you will invest the money *before* you pay the tax. The invested money will be allowed to accumulate and compound, tax sheltered, until you withdraw it. At that time, you the pay the tax on the money as you withdraw it in retirement. Accounts that use pre-tax money include many retirement accounts, such as a 401k/403b, some IRAs (Individual Retirement Arrangements), or the HSP plan (Health Savings Plan), which acts like an IRA. There are several advantages to using a pre-tax retirement account. The first is that because you do not pay tax before it is placed into the retirement account/HSP account, it leaves a larger pool of money to grow tax sheltered. The capital gains and dividends are not taxed while in the account because of the tax-advantaged status of the retirement account. The second is that by contributing to a pre-tax retirement account or HSP plan, you will lower your taxable income for the year. This may even mean being taxed at a lower rate if it drops your income to a lower tax bracket. When the tax is due in retirement, many professionals are generally in a lower tax bracket. This means further money savings by deferring the tax payment until retirement.

If it is **post-tax money**, you invest the money *after* you pay the tax. This includes retirement accounts like a Roth IRA. The benefit of the post-tax retirement account is that you will never pay taxes on the money again. Any proceeds or gains will be tax-free later, when you withdraw the money in retirement.

**Tax-advantaged accounts** are accounts that do not tax the capital gains, distributions, or dividends while the money is inside of the account. These include retirement accounts and health savings plans (which are really stealth IRA retirement accounts). By not having to pay tax on the dividends, distributions, or capital gains, the money can compound faster than if you were to pay taxes on the earnings each year. You can buy and sell the investments as many times as you want, to lock in the gains, without being taxed, as long as the money remains in the account. Tax-advantaged accounts are the best place to hold investments that will be taxed at your normal income rate, like bonds and REITS. These will be discussed later.

**Tax-disadvantaged accounts** are just as they sound—no tax breaks. Any gains will be taxed at the capital gains rate when you sell the investment and lock in the gain. Dividends and distributions, too, will be taxed. These accounts include savings accounts, certificates of deposit (CD), and regular brokerage investment accounts. Anything that is not held in a retirement or HSP account is in a tax-disadvantaged account. The proceeds from these accounts are taxed at either your normal tax rate (up to 39.6%) for items like savings accounts, CD earnings, and REIT distributions, and bond dividends. Or they are taxed at a capital gains rate of up to 20% (based on your tax bracket) on gains from stock sales or dividends.

Earlier, it was recommended that you *diversify* your investments. This is also true when it comes to tax strategies. It is a good plan to have some money in pre-tax and some in post-tax investments. That way, if the government decides to change its tax laws or raise taxes, not all of your investments will be affected.

## PORTFOLIO DIVERSIFICATION

The big goal of investing is **diversification**. This means that you want to decrease your risk of losing money while increasing your investment returns by acquiring different types of investments. If you have a huge rate of return with a large profit, but then lose the money as the market changes, it doesn't do you much good. This is especially true for your retirement funds.

Diversification means that you don't stick all of your money into one or two asset classes. By spreading your money around into different investment types, you are spreading out the risk of all those investments going bad at the same time and subsequently losing all of your money.

There are a few ways to decrease your investment risk. In this section, I'll discuss three of them: asset diversification, dollar cost averaging (DCA), and asset class diversification. Tax diversification, which we just discussed, is the way to spread out the risk from a change in tax rates.

### *ASSET DIVERSIFICATION*

If you were investing in only one asset class, such as stocks, you would diversify by holding numerous stocks. Why more than only one or two stocks? If you purchase only one "hot" stock, it may skyrocket for a while and make you lots of money. Then the market changes and the stock price falls back below where you purchased it. Your entire portfolio has now lost money. But on the other hand, if you had 100 stocks in your portfolio, and one or two stocks lost value while the others remained stable, your account balance would not see a drastic change because the other stocks help to buoy the value of the portfolio. Many experts recommend investing as broadly as possible and not attempting to beat the market with one particular stock. If you can match the overall percentage return on investment of the S&P 500, you are doing better than 95% of investors. One of the best ways to diversify your portfolio is through a broad-based stock market fund where the fund "owns" a wide array of the stocks that are available on the market or even a total stock market index fund, which will own shares of all the stocks in the US stock market.

## DOLLAR COST AVERAGING

Dollar cost averaging (DCA) is where you purchase small amounts of the same investment over long periods of time. This is how you've been investing if you invest through your 401k at work. Each paycheck you have a small amount taken out and invested into assets in your 401k. Through DCA, you can be assured that you are never buying all of your investment at peak price.

## ASSET CLASS DIVERSIFICATION

You can also add diversification by purchasing different asset classes such as stocks, bonds, commodities, real estate, and so on. **Modern Portfolio Theory** was described by Harry Markowitz in 1959 and won a Nobel Prize in Economics in 1990. The theory states that investors are risk averse, and given two investments that make the same rate of return, investors would always choose the one with the least amount of risk if everything else was equal. So an investor has a level of risk that is acceptable to him or her, and by investing in different asset classes like bonds, stocks, and real estate, it is possible to decrease the overall portfolio risk while maintaining the level of return. If you had a choice between two portfolios that each had a 9% return, but one portfolio had a 2% risk that it would lose its value and the other had a 50% risk, you would pick the portfolio with the 2% risk. This brings us to a discussion of asset class correlation.

**Asset class correlation** is how closely two classes of assets will move together. So if, let's say, stocks go up, are bonds expected to go up, stay the same, or fall? Asset correlation values are between 1 and -1. If two classes have a value close to +1, they move in tandem. So when one goes up, the other goes up. The opposite is true for those with -1. With Modern Portfolio Theory, by using those classes that move in opposite directions to each other or one that stays the same while the other moves, you can decrease your level of risk of the portfolio losing value while maintaining the expected rates of return.

In general, stocks and bonds do not correlate well. This means that if stocks move higher in value, bonds may not move or may move lower. Real estate tends to correlate poorly with most other asset classes. By utilizing those assets which have poor correlation to each other, you can better diversify your portfolio and insulate against losses. So by holding stocks, bonds, and some real estate, you may be able to create a portfolio with significantly less risk than one that has all stocks or all bonds. You should know that these correlations can change over time depending on the financial climate. You can go to www.morningstar.com to check out the present correlation values of asset classes for the last few months if you are so inclined.

### TAKEAWAYS

- Determine the amount you need to save by retirement by taking 80% of your current income and dividing it by .04 for a rough estimate.
- Pre-tax money is invested before you pay the tax due and has the advantages of lowering your taxable income for the year while leaving a larger pool of money to compound. Tax is paid when you make withdrawals in retirement. It is associated with certain retirement accounts, including 401k/403b and traditional IRAs.
- Post-tax money is invested after you have paid the tax. If the money is in a retirement account, you never pay tax on the money again. Investment accounts other than retirement accounts only use post-tax money.
- Tax-advantaged accounts include retirement accounts and health savings plans.
- Diversification is the name of the game. You can diversify through asset diversification, dollar cost averaging, and, asset correlation diversification. Also diversify your tax strategies. The goal is to lower the overall portfolio risk while maintaining or boosting returns.

### TO-DO LIST

- ☐ Determine "your number" for retirement.
- ☐ Evaluate your portfolio for diversification.

# CHAPTER 5

# RETIREMENT ACCOUNTS

Professionals know that they need to invest their money for retirement. But many do not understand why they are investing in what. Some will buy only one or two stocks that had the best performance the previous year in their retirement accounts, others will buy all gold, and some buy all bonds. Some will invest through IRAs, others only through a 401k, some only in annuities, and some through whatever vehicle their financial planner tells them to use. By getting educated, it may keep professionals from losing a lot of money to worthless investment vehicles or poor advice.

The most common retirement accounts that you will encounter are discussed below. Which type you use depends on a bunch of factors, including which plans are offered at your workplace, if your workplace is for-profit or not-for-profit, if you are self-employed, and how much money you make. This chapter will look at the following topics:

- 401k/403b
- Roth IRA
- Traditional IRA (Individual Retirement Arrangement)
- SEP IRA/SOLO 401k
- Target Date Funds
- Summing Up Retirement Accounts
- High-Deductible Health Savings Plans (Stealth IRA)
- Annuities

# 401k/403b

One of the best places to start investing is to maximize your **401k** (if employed by a "for-profit" business) or **403b** (if employed by a "not-for-profit" business) retirement account contributions, if your employer offers it. Pre-tax money is deposited into a tax-advantaged retirement account and reduces your taxable income for the year. This is a good tax strategy for shielding money from taxes. The maximum contribution for 2017 is $18,000. If you are over 50 years old, you can stash away an extra $6,000 "catch up" amount. Understand that you will pay tax on the money when you withdraw it in retirement. But you will most likely be in a lower tax bracket than you are while in practice and get some tax savings.

Another great benefit to contributing to a 401k/403b occurs if your practice offers an **employer match**. This is money contributed to your account by your employer, usually up to 3%–6% of your salary for the year or a set amount like $1,000, which "matches" your contribution amount to your 401K/403b. Not all practices have this, but if they do, it's free money. The match is in addition to the $18,000 maximum that you can personally contribute. Many employers will spread the match amount out over the entire year. So if you contribute the maximum amount to the 401k in the first half of the year, and none in the second half, then you will receive only half of the match amount. Make sure of the practice's policy. Do not miss out on this free money. Also, the match amount may be subject to vesting which is discussed below.

Some practices may do **profit sharing** as well, where a portion of the business proceeds will be distributed to employees. This does not affect your ability to contribute the maximum amount to your 401k/403b. You should know that profit sharing and 401k/403b match money may be subject to vesting.

**Vesting** means that you need to work at a practice for a certain period of time in order to keep the company match or profit sharing if you leave the company. For example, if you are vested on a five-year schedule, each year you will be entitled to keep 20% more of the money provided by the practice. So if you left your job after being there for three years, you would be able to keep 60% of the employer match and profit sharing you received over that three-year period. You keep 20% for each year you have worked. The other 40% would go back to the practice. They do this to provide you with a monetary incentive to stay at your job. Many practices have a vesting schedule, and you need to be aware of what that schedule is if you decide to change jobs. Vesting schedules only apply to the portion provided by the practice and not to your personal contribution amount.

A few final thoughts regarding 401k/403b accounts: If you leave your practice or job, it may be wise to **roll over** your 401k/403b into an IRA. This means transferring the money into another "qualified retirement account," which is the IRA (Individual Retirement Arrangement). The main reason to do this is because typically 401k/403b accounts have limited investment choices that may be poor, or the funds offered can carry higher expense fees. Rolling it over into an IRA will give you a wider selection of investments, including ones with very low fees. I will discuss why fees matter so much later. Also, if left in the company 401k/403b account, the company still has some control over that money. There have been a few incidents reported where a company "borrowed" money from the 401k and then went bankrupt. You also need to understand that 401k/403b accounts are usually protected from creditors, while IRA accounts are not. In many states, however, the laws have changed to also protect IRAs from creditors if you are sued or enter bankruptcy. You will need to check on your state's laws and decide accordingly if it makes sense to roll it over. There are no limits to the amount of 401k/403b that can be rolled over to an IRA. If you do roll it over, roll it directly to another company. *Never* get a check sent to you or you may end up with stiff penalties and taxes for improperly transferring the money.

One last note about company plans. If your company offers its stock as part of your 401k/403b, do *not* buy it. The reason is simple. If your company goes belly up, not only do you lose your job, but you also lose a part of your retirement account. So stay far away from your company's stock if it is offered—unless of course it is a stock option. Those are different story, as it is a type of deferred compensation and may be a great added benefit.

# ROTH IRA

A Roth IRA is a post-tax retirement account, which again means you put the money into the account after you have paid tax on it. Because you have already paid tax, all of the earnings will be tax-free at withdrawal in retirement. This is especially useful early on in your career if you are in a lower tax bracket than you will probably be in retirement. However, there are income caps on contributions. The adjusted gross income upper limits for 2017 are $133,000 for singles and $196,000 for married couples. You should contribute while you are able. The maximum contribution per person for 2017 is $5,500/year unless you are older than 50, and then it is $6,500. You can contribute to a Roth IRA for the tax year up until the tax is due the following April.

Another great feature of this account is that Roth IRAs do not have required mandatory withdrawals in retirement like an IRA does. That means that you can pass Roth IRAs on to heirs and the money will be tax-free. You can also continue contributing to Roth IRAs even if you are older than 70½ as long as you are still working. And if you have a non-working spouse, he or she can contribute to a Roth IRA based on your income level.

# TRADITIONAL IRA (INDIVIDUAL RETIREMENT ARRANGEMENT)

A **traditional IRA** can be a pre-tax or post-tax account (these are also referred to as a deductible and a non-deductible IRA, respectively). Contributing to a deductible IRA (pre-tax) can lower your taxable income up to a certain level. The maximum contribution for a traditional IRA for 2017 is $5,500, with an additional $1,000 "catch-up" for anyone over 50 years old. The unfortunate issue is that the tax-shielding benefit is lost with incomes over $72,000 for singles and $119,000 for married couples if you have a retirement plan at work. However, if your spouse does not have a plan at work but you do, your spouse can contribute and see some tax shielding if the combined income is less than $196,000, even if he or she doesn't work. Once you reach your practice years, you may be over these income levels. At that point it becomes a non-deductible IRA and uses "post-tax" money.

Once you lose the income tax shielding and it is a non-deductible IRA, the main purpose of the IRA becomes to shield the capital gains and dividends from taxation. Any of these retirement accounts are very beneficial to keep bonds or REITs (Real Estate Investment Trusts) in, as the dividends on these will be taxed at your regular income tax rate. However, if you pay with post-tax money, there are additional forms that you will have to fill out when setting up the account and when withdrawing from it, which makes the non-deductible IRA much more complicated and may require help from a financial professional.

Another issue with traditional IRAs is that you can no longer contribute to it once you are 70½ years old, and you will be forced to take RMDs (required mandatory distributions) at the same age. This means that even if you do not need the money, the government will force you to take a specified percentage each year.

There is a provision that allows you to roll over existing IRAs into Roth IRAs to avoid mandatory distributions in retirement, but the money gets taxed before the rollover. The amount that gets taxed will be added to your overall income for that year. So you need to be in a low tax bracket and have a long time horizon until you need the money in order for it to make sense to do a **Roth IRA conversion**.

Estate planning may be a reason to do the Roth IRA conversion. Money in an IRA has mandatory withdrawals in retirement. The rate accelerates, as you get older, in order to force you to pay tax on the money before you die. This means that even if you do not need the money, you will be forced to take the money and pay tax on it. But if the IRA is rolled over to a Roth IRA before retirement, you do not have to tap into this money unless you need it, which allows you to will the Roth IRA to future generations. If you need to, you can also reverse the Roth IRA back to a traditional IRA, but there are some tax and legal issues involved, so you would want to talk to your tax professional, CPA, or financial/estate planner about them. There are many other items to consider if you decide to do a Roth IRA conversion, which will not be discussed here. This is where your CPA, tax attorney, or financial planner can help you.

You can open most IRAs yourself by going online or calling an investment house like Vanguard or Fidelity. They will help you set up the account. This is also true of all the retirement accounts that will be discussed in this book. But you must already know how much you are eligible to contribute. The investment house will not help you to determine this.

## SEP IRA/SOLO 401k

The SEP IRA/Solo 401k accounts are available for professionals who are self-employed, such as independent contractors, consultants, or physicians doing locum tenens. These two retirement accounts allow you to contribute significantly more money than you can using a Roth IRA or a traditional IRA, because you get to be both the employer and the employee. The SEP IRA can be used for very small practices with only a handful of employees, and the Solo 401k can be used for only one self-employed person or with one employee who is your spouse. Because the amount of money put into the SEP IRA must be the same percentage for all employees, not just the professional, they are generally too expensive to do in the case of more than one or two employees. So I will discuss the SEP IRA and the Solo 401K with the assumption that there is only the professional and no employees.

A **SEP IRA** is a Simplified Employee Pension. (Some call it a "self-employed plan" to remember that it is usually for those who are self-employed.) This plan is similar to a 401k in that the money is pre-tax and lowers your taxable income for that year. The bonus to a SEP is that you can contribute in 2017 up to 25% of your income or up to $54,000, whichever is less. The downside to this plan is that you must contribute the same "employer contribution" percentage to all employees' accounts, including your own, but are only required to do so after an employee has been there for three years. So the SEP is most useful if you are self-employed with a consulting business or doing locum tenens, if you only have one or two employees, or if you have high employee turnover. The plan does not have to be funded each year if you do not have the funds available. An upside is that if you have a 401k/403b from a practice, but also do consulting as a secondary side business, you can contribute the maximum amount to both, providing the jobs are at separate business entities.

A **SOLO 401k** is a plan, which is similar to a 401k that includes a maximum "employee" contribution of $18,000 or $24,000 if you are over 50 years old for 2017. There is also an "employer" contribution of up to 25% of your salary for a combined maximum employee + employer contribution of $54,000 for 2017. The rules are similar to those of the regular 401k. If you have a spouse who works with you, you may still use this, but if you have employees other than your spouse, you will be ineligible for the Solo 401k.

If you have another job that offers you a 401k, you may not double-dip with a Solo 401k. It's one or the other. If you are under the income threshold, you can still contribute to a deductible IRA (which will lower your income level) or a Roth IRA.

## TARGET DATE FUNDS

As their name implies, these funds are based on when you plan to retire. They are becoming more popular in 401k/403b plans and tend to have lower fees than many mutual funds. These funds take into account how many years you have until retirement and invest accordingly. They get rid of the guesswork for novice investors or those who don't want to be bothered with portfolio management. However, these funds can be under-aggressive or over-aggressive compared with your risk comfort level. For example, if you have a comfort level for taking more investment risk, the target date fund closest to your retirement date may be invested in too many bonds and not enough stocks for your liking. You need to look into what the target date fund is invested in at different time periods until the target retirement date to determine if it compares with the level of risk you prefer, meaning the amount of stocks compared with bonds and cash. They change asset allocations the closer you get to retirement, resulting in fewer stocks and more bonds and cash. This means that if you prefer to take on more risk, then you should probably pick a time horizon that is further out from your retirement date so that the fund is invested in more stocks and in fewer bonds. The fund asset mix should be easily found on the Internet or through your retirement plan administrator.

For example, say you are an investor who prefers to take on more risk via more exposure to stocks and you are looking at the target date fund dated

## RETIREMENT ACCOUNT LIMITS FOR 2017

| | MAX CONTRIBUTION/ Over age 50 | MAX INCOME LIMIT Single/married | PRE-TAX vs. POST-TAX | Comments |
|---|---|---|---|---|
| **ROTH IRA** | $5,500/$6,500 | $132,000/$194,000 | POST | No Required Mandatory Distributions (RMD) at age 70½ |
| **401k 403b** | $18,000/$24,000 (up to $53,000 including profit sharing) | N/A | PRE | Look for Vesting Schedule and Employer Match |
| **TRADITIONAL IRA** | $5,500/$6,500 | $71,000/ $118,000 (If you have plan at work) No income limit if no plan at work | PRE or POST (depends on income level) | Can do Roth IRA conversion if lower tax bracket and long time to retirement |
| **SEP IRA** | Lesser of $53,000 or 25% income No over 50 catch-up | N/A | PRE | Must contribute same % for all employees. May also contribute to a separate 401k at another business |
| **SOLO 401k** | Lesser of $53,000 or 25% of income/over 50 add $6,000 | N/A | PRE | Only you +/- your spouse |

the closest to your retirement. It is invested in 20% bonds and 10% cash and only 70% stocks. You may have 20 years to go until retirement and want a more aggressive portfolio, invested in 90% stocks, only 10% bonds, and no cash. So you may need to pick a target date fund with a retirement date that is further out to capture the amount of stocks vs. bonds you want. Just because you're retiring in, let's say, 2040 does not mean you can't pick the fund for 2050.

The fund will change the mix of assets as you get closer to retirement. You need to check out the **glide path** of the fund. This refers to when and how the fund takes you out of stocks and into bonds and cash. Why does this matter? If the glide path is over-aggressive or under-aggressive, you may have issues with your retirement money: either having too many risky investments at retirement or investments that aren't getting you close enough to your retirement goals. For example, the fund has you invested in 90% stocks and 10% bonds while you are working. Then three years prior to retirement it suddenly takes you out of the majority of your stocks and into bonds. Just before the switch, the market tanks like it did in 2007–2008. You may have just lost a considerable amount of your retirement account. You may not have enough time to make it up before retirement, forcing you to delay your plans. If, however, they switch you out of your stocks too early, you may be losing out on significant portion of income from the stocks. You need to make sure there is a gentle transition between assets as you near retirement. If the glide does not match what you want, then look for a target date fund further out or closer than your actual retirement date. And if you still can't find what you want, you may need to pick a different fund and manage the transition yourself or via a financial advisor.

You also need to understand that if you choose a target date fund, the fund does the diversification for you. You do not want to get a target date fund and also have other funds or assets or you will actually be less diversified, because you will be doubling up on some of the assets. It's one or the other.

## SUMMING UP RETIREMENT ACCOUNTS

So to sum up, which retirement account you use really depends on several items. Do you have a retirement plan offered at work? How high is your income level? You may be disqualified from several options based on income. And are you self-employed? If unsure what you can contribute to, contact a tax advisor or financial planning professional for help.

Here's a recap of plans:

- Plans you can use if employed: 401k (for-profit) or 403b (not-for-profit)
- Plans you can use if your income is below $131,000 for singles or $193,000 if married: Roth IRA or a Deductible Traditional IRA
- Plans you can use if you are self-employed: SEP IRA or Solo 401k
- Plan you can use if you are in a lower tax bracket now than in retirement: Roth IRA.
- Plan you can use if you are in a higher tax bracket now than in retirement: 401k/403b, IRA, SEP IRA, Solo 401k if income levels allow to lower income tax, and pay tax in retirement (preferably at a lower tax bracket):

IRA, SEP IRA, Solo 401k, and Roth IRA accounts can be set up through your personal financial advisor or investment houses. The fees may be higher if you set these up through your financial advisor, depending on his or her fee structure, than through the low-fee investment houses. But if you are using an investment house, you will need to already know if you are eligible for the account you are trying to open. Some investment houses may not charge fees for the fund purchase or even to set up the accounts. You should be aware that there are still expense fees from the funds themselves, which I will discuss in chapter 6, "WHAT TO INVEST IN?"

A final thought about retirement accounts. In general, if you are 59½ or older, you are allowed to withdraw money from them without penalty. If you are younger than that, you have to pay penalties for early withdrawals.

There are some exceptions to that rule, but they will not be discussed here. For the sake of your retirement funds, you should proceed as if you can't withdraw any money until the approved retirement age. Also, don't forget that many retirement accounts will force RMD or "required mandatory distributions" by age 70½.

## "HIGH-DEDUCTIBLE" HEALTH SAVINGS PLANS/ STEALTH IRA

A quick note about Health Savings Plans. They are most often associated with high-deductible health insurance plans. These plans are definitely worth doing. Some people worry that if they need surgery or some other procedure, they would be better off using a regular-deductible health plan instead of going with a high-deductible plan. That happened to me. I needed surgery and decided to switch from a high-deductible plan to the lower-deductible plan. But after everything was over, I crunched the numbers and realized I spent just as much money as if I had kept the high-deductible plan, and I wasn't able to stash away any money in the Health Savings Plan for that year.

I am only talking about the Health Savings Plan (HSP) that never expires. Please do not confuse this with the run-of-the-mill Flexible Savings Plan that the government takes away each year if you don't use it. The HSP plan lowers your taxable income level for the year like a 401k does and allows you to invest a large portion of the money in an investment account. It's really a stealth IRA because it is both tax-advantaged and pre-tax. The money can be used tax-free for many health-related expenses, including long-term care or can be withdrawn in retirement, like an IRA. According to a study done by Fidelity in 2015, a 65-year-old couple with Medicare, who retired in 2015, will spend $245,000 on average during retirement for health-related expenses, not including long-term care or nursing care. If you do not need the money now, you are better off investing the amount and not touching it until retirement, even if you have a health-related expense. But in the meantime, keep all of the receipts for any healthcare-related expenses that you pay prior to retirement. Then when you withdraw the money in retirement for anything that is not healthcare-related, the amount of the receipts you have saved over the years would be tax-free. The remainder of the proceeds that you withdraw without receipts in retirement will be taxed like IRA distributions unless used for health-related expenses.

## ANNUITIES

I have decided to discuss annuities in this chapter, as some people will consider annuities for a stream of income in retirement. Annuities are an investment strategy where you give an insurance company a lump sum of money or periodic payments over several years, and in return you are guaranteed a monthly income stream usually for the rest of your life or even part of your spouse's life. The income can begin immediately, as with an **immediate annuity,** or in several years as with a **deferred annuity**. The purpose is to create an income stream, which can help alleviate some retirees' fears of running out of money before their death. Social Security is a type of annuity. Annuities can mitigate your longevity risk, which is the risk of you outliving your money supply. The catch is that once you give the money to the insurance company, if you need the money for whatever reason, you cannot touch it again for a long time without incurring large penalties. Generally the penalties disappear once you are past the surrender period, which could be longer than five to ten years.

There are several types of annuities, including fixed, variable, and indexed. **Fixed annuities** guarantee you a fixed rate of return over the period of benefits. Usually the longer you defer the benefits and the older you are when your start receiving annuity payments, the more monthly benefit you receive. **Variable annuities** invest in mutual funds and your benefits are based on the returns of those investments. Variable annuities frequently guarantee that you will get at least your initial investment back. **Indexed annuities** are pegged to an index like the S&P 500. The annuity may guarantee you a percentage, let's say, 50%, of the market returns up to a certain percentage, like 12%, even if the market is up 30%. In return for giving up some of the market returns, you are immune from any losses if the market enters a downturn and the annuity loses money. These annuities usually guarantee a return of your initial investment plus an additional percentage rate. Any of these annuities can be either immediate or deferred annuities. It is very important to check the creditworthiness and financial strength of the insurance company to guarantee you will get your money back as promised.

One reason people choose annuities is for the peace of mind of having a predictable income stream that will last until they die. Annuities may also come with a death benefit to your heirs if you have not yet begun receiving distributions prior to your death. And lastly, they have tax-deferred growth like an IRA, but the tax is due when you start receiving benefits. Because annuities have their own tax benefits, they should never be held in an IRA or 401k.

But there are risks that come with annuities. If you start receiving benefits before your death, at your death your heirs will receive nothing unless the benefit was guaranteed to last for your spouse as well. Annuities are illiquid and tie up a large chunk of your money. In the event that you need that money and you have not passed the surrender date, you will have to pay stiff penalties to access that money. Also, if you are less than 59½ years old, you may have to pay the IRS penalties as well.

Annuities are sold through insurance companies, brokerages, banks, and even some investment houses. The down side is that a very large portion of the annuity payment goes as a commission to the person who sold you the annuity. So right off the top, you have lost investment power. The income stream provided by the annuity can be quite small for the amount invested. Let's say you invest $50,000. Depending on the interest rates and length of time until you receive benefits, you may only get $350 per month back. That's only $4,200 per year, not much to live on, and it may not give you the peace of mind you are looking for. Also, you should know that annuities can have a 10% commission, charge 2%–3% in annual fees, and have large surrender penalties, all of which eat away at your income stream.

If you want to purchase an annuity, I recommend discussing the appropriateness with a fee-based fiduciary financial planner who does not sell annuities. In doing so, you are able to have a bias-free conversation about what is best for your situation. Also, as with any investment, make sure you choose an annuity with low fees. Low-fee issuers of annuities include Vanguard, Fidelity, Schwab, and T. Rowe Price.

In periods with low interest rates, as they were in 2016, purchasing a fixed annuity is usually a poor choice. This is because you will be locked into that low interest rate forever. If interest rates rise to a much higher level, it may then be worth considering annuities if you must have a steady income stream to help you sleep at night. Otherwise, a low-fee index fund may make more sense. As with all investments, be aware of the upsides and downsides to whatever you choose.

## TAKEAWAYS

- The 401k retirement account is used at for-profit businesses and the 403b is used at not-for-profit organizations. There may be an employer match, which is free money you should not pass up. Be aware of any vesting schedules that might be in place if you decide to leave your current job. You can contribute up to $18,000, which will lower your taxable income for the year.
- Traditional IRA contribution limits are $5,500 and can lower your taxable income for the year if under $119,000 income limit.
- Real Estate Investment Trusts (REITs) and bonds belong in retirement accounts, if possible, as they are taxed at your normal income tax level. Stocks are taxed at a lower capital gains rate.
- SEP IRA and Solo 401k are available for professionals who are the only employee of the business.
- A target date fund provides you with diversification. Do not also invest in other mutual funds or you ruin the diversification. Check out the asset investments and glide path to make sure they meet your risk tolerance. If they don't meet it, consider a target date further out from or closer to your retirement date.
- Health Savings Plans act like stealth IRAs. Keep receipts for health-related expenses, and the amount of those receipts will be tax-free in retirement.
- Annuities are best avoided unless you have particular reasons to buy one. They come with expensive commissions and fees and are generally poor investment choices in low interest rate environments.

## TO-DO LIST

☐ Determine the amount you need for retirement if you haven't already done so.

☐ Know if you are using a tax-advantaged or disadvantaged account. Put investments that will be taxed at your normal income tax rate in the tax-advantaged accounts, if you can.

☐ Maximize 401k/403b contributions to decrease taxable income, using pre-tax money.

☐ If there is an employer match, contribute over the entire year to get the company's entire match. Be aware of any vesting schedule.

☐ If you leave your practice or job, strongly consider rolling over your 401k/403b to an IRA.

☐ Contribute to a Roth IRA if under the income level limit.

# CHAPTER 6

# WHAT TO INVEST IN?

R etirement accounts are only the baskets or containers in which you hold assets like stocks, bonds, gold, real estate, and so on. What you invest in depends mainly on when you need the money from the investment. There is the **short term** of less than one or two years, **intermediate term** of three-to-five years, and **long term** of more than five years. Different **asset classes** are used depending on when the money is needed. The goal is to get the best return while preserving the money you have.

This chapter will look at the following topics:

- Asset Classes
- What To Invest In?
- Asset Diversification Revisited
- Portfolio Rebalancing
- Keeping Costs Low
- Mutual Funds
- ETF (Exchange-Traded Funds)
- Index Funds

## ASSET CLASSES

Asset classes are groups of items with tradable value that you invest in and include stocks, bonds, commodities (gold, oil, wheat, hogs, etc.), cash, and real estate. There are other "assets," items that have value, but the ones mentioned above are the ones most commonly discussed with respect to investing. Mutual funds are not asset classes. They are a basket that holds the assets. So if you have a stock mutual fund, the mutual fund is a basket that holds multiple stocks. If you have a stock mutual fund that's in your IRA, it's like having a basket, the mutual fund, which is holding the stocks, inside another basket, the IRA.

## WHAT TO INVEST IN?

Anything needed in the next six-to-12 or even 24 months should be held as cash or cash equivalent. "Cash equivalent" means it is "liquid," that it can immediately be turned into cash and is assured of maintaining its value. Examples are savings or money market deposit accounts. If you lose your job and need money now to pay rent and buy groceries, having your rainy day fund tied up in 30-year bonds or volatile stocks is probably not going to work out so well. Even a six-month CD might not be the best choice if you need the money now. So make sure your rainy day fund is available immediately as cash, even if this means you aren't making significant returns on your money. The rainy day fund is *not there to generate money*; its sole purpose is to be there for protection should something financially bad happen.

For money needed in six-to-24 months, plan on having it in cash equivalents like savings accounts, CDs, short-term savings bonds, money market accounts, or ultra short bonds or Treasuries that mature in the time frame in which you need the money. These need to be safe, secure, and guaranteed not to lose value. The FDIC (Federal Deposit Insurance Corporation) guarantees some of these. I will discuss each of these in detail later.

For the money you need in three-to-five years, I will discuss using things like longer-term CDs and savings bonds, short-term Treasuries, or intermediate-term corporate bonds. All of these have maturities between three-to-five years and are much more stable than stocks, providing you hold them to maturity. Again, you need to choose the maturity length that corresponds to when you may need to use the money. For example, if you know you need the money in six months, choose a CD that matures in six months. Otherwise, when you do need the money, it might not be available.

That is what happened to some physicians who were nearing retirement in 2008. Stocks can be very volatile and can lose considerable value as they did in the recession of 2007–2008. Older physicians, who had a significant amount of their money in stocks when the depression hit, lost almost half of their account values. They didn't have the money they needed for the next three-to-five years in the appropriate assets, like bonds or CDs. Stocks tanked, and by the time the economy had straightened out, they had to prolong their retirement plans, waiting for their accounts to recover. It took until 2013 for the stock market to recover to the 2007 level. They ended up working much longer than they had originally planned.

Any money that will not be needed for at least five years or more should be placed into stocks. Why only the money needed in more than five years? You are looking for money preservation first and appreciation second. It doesn't help to make vast amounts of money if you end up losing it all. The further out you go in time when looking at stock market returns, the better chance you have of getting consistently positive gains. Of course that doesn't guarantee future performance. For shorter time periods, which were less than five years, the greater the chance the market had of having some time periods with negative returns. The further out you go (for example, more than five years), the more likely that the average stock market returns for a particular period will be positive. So the least amount of time you should plan to hold stocks is five years to allow time for capital appreciation and to decrease the chances that you will lose money from a fall in stock prices. You should know that over 40% of the stock market returns are made from reinvestment of the dividends, not just the price appreciation. If you buy stocks, you should plan on reinvesting the dividends or you are missing out on almost half of the gains.

Now you say, okay, what if I'm 64 years old and getting ready for retirement? Do I really want part of my money in stocks? Well, yes. The money you don't need for five years or more should be in stocks. What happens if you retire at 65 and you live to 100? If you place all of your money into bonds or cash, you will probably outlive your supply. If you don't need some of that money for 30 years, it had better be earning you a good return.

If you are young and just starting out in your career, you may not need to worry as much about the three-to-five-year time period. While you are working, you have a flow of cash from your job, so you may not need to have much money set aside for the three-to-five-year time period, unless you plan on making a large outlay of cash or decide to leave your job. For example, if you don't have children who are about to go to college, then you won't need to worry about having money available to pay for your children's college tuition. So it may be appropriate to place the majority of your savings into stocks. Also, if the stock market falls, you have plenty of time, possibly 30 to 40 years or more before retirement, for your portfolio to recover while you are still earning a paycheck. Lastly, since you have such a long time horizon until retirement, you want your money to be working as hard for you as it can. This means harnessing all of the power of compounding that the money can muster. And since over longer time periods, stocks tend to be one of the best-performing asset classes, having a significant portion of your investments in stocks is usually the best thing you can do. Keep in mind that you still need your rainy day fund fully funded.

After you have decided how much money you need for your different time periods, you need to determine what percentage that translates into for each asset class. You may determine that 10% should be in cash equivalents, 10% should be in bonds, and 80% in stocks. This will help guide you on how much you invest into each asset class as you pick your investments. These percentages will also guide your portfolio management in the future.

The above assets for the different time periods are only suggestions. It is up to you and your financial "team," if you have one, to decide what is the best strategy for the current market. If the interest rates are low like they are in the current market and the Fed is expected to raise rates, then you might not want to lock yourself into low-interest, long-term bonds. The same is true for the stock market. If the stock market is at its peak, you may not want to be throwing new money at it to try and "catch it." Because, the chances are good that you have already missed the upswing and should probably wait for a pull back before investing or use dollar cost averaging.

## ASSET DIVERSIFICATION REVISITED

It's helpful to remember that you can lower your portfolio's risk while increasing the rate of return by using as many diversification strategies as you can. For example, someone decides he wants to own a mix of stocks, bonds, and real estate in his portfolio to utilize asset class diversification and poor asset correlation. He does so by purchasing a total stock market fund and a broad-based bond fund but does it by putting a little money each month into his investments. He also invests in a medical building REIT and a shopping mall REIT. He has incorporated asset class diversification, poor asset correlation, dollar cost averaging, and single asset diversification. So now, if several stocks fall in price, the chances are good that he has another investment in his portfolio that is doing well and can offset the fall of the stock prices. It may be that one of his asset classes, such as bonds, is doing so well that it has gained significant value and proportion in his portfolio. What should he do about that? Does he keep watching it grow in value or should he sell some of the bonds and lock in the gains? This question brings us to a discussion of portfolio rebalancing.

## PORTFOLIO REBALANCING

Once you have diversified as much as possible, you need to forget about it. That means you stop "market timing" by moving your money around trying to catch the next big thing. You may have heard financial pundits recommend that buy-and-hold is not appropriate. The pundits are talking about if you own individual stocks. If you have only one or two stocks, you had better not hold them and forget them. You need to do research on your companies each week to see if there is something happening to the company that might impact the stock price. Most physicians I know don't have that kind of time. Besides, it's too risky to only own one or two stocks. It's better for you to go with a broad-based stock market fund with very low fees and just hold it. By having a broad, well-diversified portfolio comprised of many different assets, which you hold, you will avoid trading on emotion, decrease the amount of buying and selling, and keep transaction costs low. Every time you buy and sell a stock, you create transaction fees, which significantly eat away at your profits. If you feel the need to trade individual stocks, keep less than 5% of your money that you will *never need* in a trading account, but no more. Each year, compare your account values. My bet is that the well-diversified, buy-and-hold account has the higher value. However, you periodically need to evaluate your investments and **rebalance** the portfolio.

Let's discuss how to rebalance. The first step is to figure out how much money you will keep in bonds, stocks, real estate, and so on and come up with the percentages that you need in each. For example, let's say you need $5,000/month for expenses, and you have $500,000 to invest. So the money you need for the next year, $60,000, should be in cash equivalents. This is an overly conservative number. If you are currently working, you may opt to have much less held in cash because you have cash coming in each month from your job. The money for the next three years, $180,000, you keep in bonds. The rest will be in stocks. So you will have around 10% in cash equivalents, 30%–40% in bonds, and 50%–60% in stocks. But, you decide that because you are still working with a continuous influx of cash and have a great disability policy in case you get injured, you don't really need to have as much held in cash or bonds and decide to keep more in stocks. So you choose to have 5% in cash, 10% bonds, and 85% in stocks. You invest your money according to the decided percentages.

The second step is this: once a month, once a quarter, or once a year, whatever fits your schedule, look at your investments and see if the percentages are out of alignment. For example, you say you need 10% in bonds and 85% in stocks. You check your investments at the end of the predetermined time period and realize that you have 90% stocks and only 5% in bonds because stocks were doing so well. Do you leave it alone because the stocks are on fire? No. You *rebalance* it to bring it back to 10/85 either by buying more bonds or by selling some stocks to buy bonds. By doing this you take emotion out of your investments and you can lock in stock gains. Doing it this way avoids selling the stocks at their lowest. If you instead hold onto the stocks because they are on fire, the likelihood is high that you will hold on to them until they have reversed course and are losing money. Multiple studies have shown time and time again that this is what happens if people don't have a predetermined plan. Now if bonds happen to start moving significantly higher, and you have not followed the rebalancing plan, you only have 5% of your money working for you instead of the 10% you had predetermined. You just lost out on extra gains you would have otherwise had.

Once you have a plan for investing your long-term money, stick to it. If you are well diversified in something like a total stock market fund and the stock market begins to tank like it did in late 2007–2008, do not touch your money. If the market is in free fall, you would be better off sitting tight and doing nothing or buying more of whatever is going down as you rebalance instead of selling the ones that are too high in value if the asset proportions in the portfolio are out of balance. If you sell your assets, you will lock in those losses. The market is likely to go back up and not to zero. The only way the market can go to zero is if all of the companies go belly up. That's not likely to happen. The rebound is generally stronger and longer than the decline. And, because you are a savvy investor, you do not have any of the money that you need in the next three-to-five years in risky investments like stocks, anyway. So you don't need to worry in the short term. You need to begin to look at market pullbacks as great buying opportunities. It's like the stock market is on sale.

Before I go into more specifics of the different investment options that I mentioned above under "Asset Classes," you need to think about whether the account you are investing in is tax-advantaged or not. Some options like corporate bonds and REITs are taxed at your normal income tax rate. These, therefore, belong in a tax-advantaged account like your retirement account to limit taxation on the distributions. Stocks, on the other hand, are taxed at the significantly lower capital gains rates and can be kept in any account.

## KEEPING COSTS LOW

Before discussing what to invest in, I want to be sure that you understand that the winning strategy is not to beat the return on investment of the stock market but to *match* it. Trying to beat the market by trading risky stocks or hiring fancy money managers may allow you to beat the market one year. However, a study by S&P Dow Jones Indices shows that even if a stock or a fund can beat the market one year, there is a very high likelihood it won't beat it again the next. In trying to do so, you will waste a lot of money and decrease your returns. Multiple studies have shown that is nearly impossible to consistently beat the market year after year. By being average and trying to simply match the average returns of the stock market, you will beat the majority of investors.

In 2008, Warren Buffett bet a top hedge fund in New York that over the ensuing years, a low-fee index fund, which I will discuss next, would outperform anything the hedge fund would invest in because of the difference they each would pay in fees. This bet took place around the time that recession hit the US markets at the end of 2007. Buffett declared that he would invest in the low-fee Vanguard 500 Index Fund, which tracks the S&P 500, and the hedge fund would invest into whatever it thought would get the best returns. At the end of ten years they would compare account values. Whoever lost would donate $1,000,000 to the winner's charity of choice. As of 2016, the eighth year of the bet, the S&P was up 85% despite the recession and subsequent recovery. The hedge fund was only up 22%. Let's briefly discuss why Warren Buffett is right and why it is so hard to beat the market even if you are a top hedge fund manager.

**Number One: Past Fund Performance.** Experienced investors agree that "past performance is no guarantee of future results." When uninformed investors are choosing investments, some try to find a fund that did really well last year or even over the last two or three years, and decide to invest in that fund because of the past performance. The problem, which multiple studies have shown, is that the funds that perform the best one year frequently end up on the bottom for performance the next. It's because more investors enter those funds due to the higher previous returns and flood them with an influx of cash. The funds becomes less nimble because they have more difficulty finding places to invest that influx of cash. They have a harder time getting the investment returns that they did when they were smaller funds and could be pickier with the investments they made.

**Number Two: Transaction Fees.** When you invest in an actively traded fund, the money manager is constantly buying and selling stocks, trying to beat the market. Every time stocks are bought or sold, transaction fees occur. Mutual funds pass these fees on to you. They don't advertise that you are paying them, but you are paying them nonetheless. The fees simply come off of your bottom line. In a study by the investment management firm Rebalance IRA, a majority of investors in mutual funds that they surveyed incorrectly thought they were paying nothing or almost nothing in fees for their mutual funds. By picking funds that keep the turnover of assets low, you will contain the transaction fees that you pay.

A gauge to the amount of transaction fees you might pay is the percentage of asset turnover for a fund. If the fund has 100% or 200% turnover, it means that the fund is buying and selling the equivalent of all of the assets or even two times the number of assets in the fund. That is a lot of transaction fees, not to mention the capital gain tax the fund and therefore you, the investor, are paying on each asset sale that is profitable. Even if you decide to trade for yourself, every time you buy or sell a stock you pay a commission if you use a brokerage house. Almost seven dollars or whatever transaction fee you are paying doesn't seem like a lot, does it? However, combine those with the fund fees and taxes, and they add up and eat away at your profits.

**Number Three: Fund Fees.** These are the fees with names like front-end load and back-end load, or 12b-1 fees. They are also known as Class A shares (front-end load) or C shares (level fees paid each year). A front-end load is a fee charged up front, which can be 2%–5.5% for the privilege of being allowed to buy the fund shares. The 12b-1 fees are annual marketing or distribution fees, so you can pay for the fund to advertise to other investors. Why would you pay loads and 12b-1fees when there are plenty of funds without them? Even if the money manager at the fund can beat the market consistently, consider this: If you pay a 4% load and the stock market is returning 8%, that fund would need to make 12% return just to break even with the market. By keeping your fund fees low, you have a better chance of being able to break even with the market and get better returns than the majority of investors.

**Number Four: Money Manager Fees.** You say, "I don't have time to manage my own accounts. So I'll pay a guy who is an 'expert' to manage them for me." There is only one problem. He, too, will generally not beat the market, may place you into funds that charge fees or loads, and then he'll take 1%–2% of your account for "managing" your money. Let's say he takes 1% for managing your account, and you pay 2% in fund fees and 2% in transaction fees. In order to beat the market, you have to get considerably higher returns than the market just to break even with it. If you really desire help, hiring a fee-based financial planner to help you may be significantly less expensive than paying 1% of your assets under management each year.

**Number Five: Taxes.** Every time you or your money manager moves your money around, if it's not in a tax-advantaged retirement account, you pay taxes on the capital gains. This even occurs when managers trade stocks inside of a fund. So if you let your money appreciate in something like a total stock market fund that has very low stock turnover, you keep the taxes low and allow the fund to appreciate in value without paying taxes on the sales of assets.

So what is your best option? The best course of action is usually to do it yourself by buying a broad-based index fund with low fees and low asset turnover that you hold for the long term, or if you think you need help, get a fee-based financial planner. If you are looking for your best option for investing in stocks, consider a broad-based total US stock market index fund or an S&P 500 index fund. The companies traded on the US stock market usually provide some international exposure because of their business abroad. If you desire more international exposure, you can look for a "non-US" broad international index fund. International stocks are significantly more risky, and it is recommended that you hold less than 20% of your stocks in international stocks due to that increased risk. But it really comes down to your risk tolerance and how long you have until retirement. You need to remember that you want money preservation first and then appreciation. If you are looking for bonds, you can hold US Treasuries, broad-based corporate intermediate bond funds, or long-term municipal bond funds. I will discuss all of these later. It is usually better to invest through a broad-based fund rather than an individual stock, bond, or other asset.

The most important key for long-term investing is to find funds with very low fees and low turnover. You are looking for funds with no loads, fees of less than 0.5%, and asset turnover of less than 100%. The lower the better. If you are investing in broad-based, low-fee, low-turnover, buy-and-hold funds and are committed to doing the rebalancing, then you shouldn't need to pay 1%–2% for someone to manage your money. If you're not committed, then consider a fee-based planner.

## MUTUAL FUNDS

A mutual fund is a basket that holds a collection of stocks, bonds, or a combination of assets along with cash. These are one of the most common "investments" inside of a retirement account. As stated above, a mutual fund is not an asset like a stock or bond, but rather it is a basket that holds a collection of those things. If you invest in a mutual fund, you pool your money with other investors to buy the stocks, bonds, and so on that are held in the mutual fund, and you share in the expenses and investment returns. Mutual funds may have a theme. For example, the fund may be a collection of international stocks or a collection of growth stocks. The name of the fund may give you an idea of what it invests in, but the best way to know is to look in the fund prospectus issued by the fund where it lists its largest holdings.

Mutual funds can be actively or passively managed. If a mutual fund is being **actively managed**, it means a manager is at the helm actively trying to outperform the market by buying or selling assets. Because of all of the buying and selling and paying for the fund manager, the expenses and fees of the funds tend to run significantly higher than for a passive fund. A **passively managed** fund only tries to match a benchmark, like the entire US stock market or the S&P 500, with minimal active trading. **Index funds** are passively managed. An index fund that is trying to match the S&P 500 will hold all 500 stocks in the S&P 500 with the same market weighting (the percentage each stock has of the overall market). Because the fund assets change only as the stocks and weighting change in the benchmark that it is mirroring, there is low asset turnover. Passively traded funds are usually a better choice than actively traded ones because they minimize fees. There are less transaction costs and taxes and less overhead for the fund manager. Fund expenses can be found on the front page of the fund prospectus or the fund's website. Passively traded funds may have fees less than 0.5%, while actively managed funds can have fees above 2%–6%. This can add up to a big swing in account values.

Let's consider the following example. You and a friend each have $100,000. You decide to invest in a passively managed index fund with 0.5% in fees, and your friend invests in an actively managed fund and pays 5% in fees. You are paying $500/year and your friend is paying $5,000/year in fees. Over 30 years, you pay $15,000 in fees. Your friend pays $150,000 in fees. Just image how much that will amount to if you also consider compounding. If you get 8% returns per year on your extra $4,500 that you are not paying in fees each year, over 30 years you will have almost $600,000 more than your friend simply by picking the passively managed fund over his actively managed one.

Let's assume, for example purposes, that his actively managed fund outperforms your index fund year after year and brings in 10% returns, while yours is making 8.5%. With the 5% in fees he is paying taken out of the returns, he is only making 5% total return, while you are making 8% per year, even though his fund is outperforming yours. At the end of 30 years, if you both invest $100,000, his actively managed account will have slightly over $430,000 while your passively managed account will have over $1,000,000. Half of your account value is secondary to fee savings. Even if you can beat the market, you will still lose. So you see, it pays to just be average.

So why do many investors choose the actively managed fund over the passive fund? Many investors will choose the actively managed funds because they incorrectly believe that a money manager will be able to consistently beat the market average. SPIVA (S&P Indices Versus Active Funds) each year compares actively managed funds vs. the S&P 500 benchmark. In 2015, 64% of the actively managed funds underperformed against the S&P for the year. This became even worse when they looked back for a ten-year time period when 85% of the actively managed funds underperformed the S&P.

Let's look again at the fees you need to avoid or minimize.

## SALES LOADS

These are fees you pay simply for the privilege of being allowed to buy into the mutual fund. These can be as high as 5.5%. I have discussed these previously. These include front-end loads (class A shares), where you pay the fee up front; Class B shares for "back-end," where you pay the fees when you leave the fund, although these have been mostly phased out; and Class C shares, where you pay a level load or an annual maintenance fee that may be more than 1%. There are also fees called 12b-1, which some funds charge so they can pay for maintenance, advertising, and so on. But there are funds that do not have these fees, including those from Vanguard or T. Rowe Price. So avoid these fees and loads; there are better options out there.

## TAXES

Every time your manager sells a stock, bond, or asset in the fund for a profit, you accumulate taxes that must be paid. You must report those gains and dividend distributions, even if they are reinvested, on your income taxes each year, unless they are in a retirement account. Also, if you sell the mutual fund for a profit, you must pay tax on that as well. So it seems logical that if there is lower fund turnover, you will be paying fewer taxes on the capital gains. If you have losses, you can "tax-harvest" those. **Tax harvesting** means that the IRS allows you to take up to $3,000 per year of investment losses to offset any capital gains you may have for that same year to save on taxes. The rest of your losses can carry over to future years and be used to offset future capital gains.

Also be aware that if you buy into a mutual fund in November or December, you will be paying taxes on any appreciation of the fund for the last year, even if you did not get to enjoy that appreciation! For example, if you pay in $5,000 in November and the taxes are $500 on that amount of those shares, you have really only invested $4,500 and paid $500 in taxes. If you are in the latter half of the year, consider waiting until January to invest in order to avoid the tax crunch.

## WRAP FEES

These are fees charged by a money manager that wrap up all fees into one fee. Be aware that some mutual funds will try to get you to pay a wrap fee that includes money for advice that they aren't providing you. Don't pay a wrap fee from a mutual fund. Go elsewhere.

To find out what fees you are paying, you need to look at the total expense ratio. This you can find on the front page of the prospectus. You really should be paying less than 0.5%. If you are paying more than that, you need to find a different fund with lower fees. You also need to find out the **total fund turnover**, which in an index fund is less than 100%. In an actively managed fund it could be 200%–300% or more. Most fees are usually listed on the front page of the prospectus or on the fund website. Look for titles like "Shareholder Fees" and "Annual Fund Operating Expenses." Also ask for the SPD (Summary Plan Description), which can contain other information that is not mentioned in the prospectus.

When investing in low-fee index funds, you should go directly to the source to avoid transaction fees. Vanguard is the leader in low-cost index funds. But others, such as Fidelity and T. Rowe Price, will offer them as well. Avoid purchasing these funds through brokers that want to charge you trading fees for transactions, such as $6.95 per trade. You can open these online or call the investment house to help you set up the account. If you buy the investment house funds from that investment house, let's say, a Vanguard fund from Vanguard, they are usually free of brokerage costs that you would pay if you bought the Vanguard fund from a discount online broker.

A downside of mutual funds is that they are only priced once a day. The prices for the funds are listed at the end of the day as the **net asset value** (NAV) and can only be traded at the close of the day. This brings me to ETFs.

## ETF (EXCHANGE-TRADED FUNDS)

If you like mutual funds, ETFs may be a better option. ETFs are similar to mutual funds, but they can be bought and sold like stocks at any time throughout the day. They are similar to an index fund in that they usually track an index and have low fees. The downside is that they commonly are traded through a discount brokerage house and trigger commissions. But they can also be purchased directly from an investment house like Vanguard or Fidelity just like a mutual fund, which may not trigger a commission. It's always best to purchase from the source, if possible.

# INDEX FUNDS

All index funds are passively managed and track a particular index such as the S&P, the Russell 2000, or even the entire stock market. They can also be more specific, such as an energy index fund that only tracks energy stocks, a tech index fund that tracks the tech stocks, or a Pacific Rim index fund that only track stocks from countries in the Pacific Rim. There are also bond indexes that track specific bond markets such as 30-year bonds. When the weighting of the assets (individual stocks or bonds) of the index changes, then the index fund buys or sells assets to rematch the market valuation that it is tracking. Because of the low asset turnover and passive management, index funds have very low fees. International index funds will tend to have slightly higher fees because they need increased oversight in volatile markets with boots on the ground to keep an eye on what is happening in the respective countries. International markets can have issues with political unrest, currency issues, and so on. Index funds can be traded as ETFs or as mutual funds.

## TAKEAWAYS

- Determine your timeframe for needing the money: one-to-two years, cash equivalents; three-to-five years, bonds and long-term CDs; more than five years, stocks.
- Diversify your assets by using different asset classes that have low correlation, by using dollar cost averaging, and by holding as many assets in each class as possible.
- Set your percentage of asset mix and rebalance monthly, quarterly, or yearly to lock in profits and maintain those percentages.
- Mutual funds and exchange-traded funds are not assets. They are the baskets that hold assets such as stocks, cash, bonds, commodities, and real estate.
- Keep transaction fees, asset turnover, and taxes low. Don't try to beat the market. Be average. You want less than 0.5% transactions fees and less than 100% asset turnover. Passively managed funds usually perform better than actively managed ones.
- Be wary of investing in a mutual fund at the end of the year. Consider investing in January to avoid taxes on gains that you have not gotten benefit from.

- ETFs are like mutual funds but can be traded throughout the day. Mutual funds can only be bought or sold at the close of the day based on the NAV (net asset value) price.

**TO-DO LIST**

☐ Determine how much money you need for the next one or two years, for three-to-five years, and more than five years in order to determine the amount you need in cash equivalents, bonds, and stocks.

☐ Begin investing in percentages equal to what you determined above. Look for low-fee index funds to minimize costs.

☐ Plan your rebalancing schedule, mark the schedule on a calendar, and rebalance according to the percentages you have determined for each asset. Don't be tempted to rebalance based on how high or low the market is. Stick to the calendar!

# CHAPTER 7

# YOU NEED THE MONEY IN LESS THAN ONE-TO-TWO YEARS

Whatever money you are going to need in the next year or two needs to be readily accessible. This means that the money must be kept in cash or cash equivalents so it is available when you need it and is guaranteed to have maintained its value. This chapter will look at the following cash and cash equivalent accounts:

- Savings Accounts
- Money Market Deposit Account vs. Money Market Mutual Fund
- CD (Certificate of Deposit)
- Short-Term Bonds

## SAVINGS ACCOUNTS

Many people have savings accounts with a bank or credit union where they park cash needed in the short term. These accounts generally provide very low interest rates, but your money is safe and guaranteed to be there up to $250,000 per account type per bank per person (FDIC guaranteed).

## MONEY MARKET DEPOSIT ACCOUNT VS. MONEY MARKET MUTUAL FUND

Many people think that a "money market account" is like a savings account on mild steroids. You need to distinguish between the money market "deposit account" and the money market "mutual fund," because they are very different and can both be called a money market account. A **money market *deposit account*** is very similar to a savings account in that is it is very liquid and FDIC-insured but tends to earn interest rates only slightly higher than a savings account. The catch for the higher interest rate is that usually there is a minimum amount that you have to invest. These can be opened via banks, investment houses, or discount brokerages.

A **money market *mutual fund*** also is a place to park short-term money, but it can be less liquid and less secure than the money market deposit account. It is not FDIC-insured. Do not confuse the two accounts. The money market mutual fund is, after all, a type of mutual fund, which usually earns higher interest than the deposit account because of increased risk. In this type of mutual fund, the fund tries to keep the share price, that is, the NAV (net asset value) at $1 instead of letting it fluctuate like a regular mutual fund. There are cautionary tales of an investing institution holding risky assets that went south, causing a money market mutual fund's investors to lose their money. But recently, the government has mandated that institutions can only invest the money in short-term, safe investments to better ensure against losses. You invest in money market funds through a discount brokerage or investment house.

Since the maturity time frames are so short for the underlying investments (less than 60 days), money market mutual funds are good in an environment of rapidly rising interest rates. This is because the money market mutual fund can quickly adjust the rate of return upward to follow the increasing interest rates.

Depending on what underlying assets the money market mutual fund is investing in, you may also get a tax break. If the fund is investing in tax-exempt municipal bonds ("munis"), which will be discussed later, you may not have to pay state and local tax and possibly no federal tax either on the gains and distributions. Otherwise, you are taxed at your normal tax rate unless the mutual fund is held in a retirement account. Taxable fund tends to carry a higher rate of return because they are not tax-exempt. But the tax-exempt money market funds tend to be better for those in the highest tax brackets because the bigger tax savings offset the smaller rate of return. You must to do the math to see if the taxable mutual fund would produce better returns for you than the tax-exempt fund and its tax savings depending on your tax bracket. You need to understand that any money invested in the money market mutual funds will be less liquid and subject to higher risk than many of the other short-term investment options.

## CD (CERTIFICATE OF DEPOSIT)

Certificates of Deposit (CDs) can be purchased at your local bank or credit union, investment house, or even some online discount brokers, and are insured by the FDIC (Federal Deposit Insurance Corporation), which means that you are guaranteed to get your money back. CDs come with a maturity date and a guaranteed interest rate. The interest rate is generally quoted as an APY (annual percentage yield), which takes into account compounding of the interest. (Of note, the APR, the annual percentage rate, does not take compounding into consideration. There can be a big swing between amounts calculated by APY and those with APR. Make sure you compare apples to apples by looking at a CD's APY compared with another CD's APY and not its APR.) Interest can be compounded yearly, quarterly, or monthly. Monthly compounding will have a higher APY than those options that compound yearly. The maturity dates can be from one month to years. For the short term you can purchase CDs for 1, 3, 6, 7, 9, or 12 months. If you prematurely withdraw the money, you will pay a penalty.

For simplicity, I will only discuss fixed-rate CDs. There are many types of CDs, but the most common is fixed rate. "Fixed-rate" means that you are guaranteed a fixed rate of return for a predetermined time period. You receive a dividend periodically until the maturity date. As with stocks, you will earn more if you reinvest the dividends because the dividend can begin to bear interest as well. The longer the time period until the maturity date, usually the higher the interest rate offered. As stated earlier, you are paying taxes at your ordinary income tax rate on the dividends, even if they are reinvested.

The biggest risk for a CD is **interest rate risk**, and this is especially true for a longer-term CD. So while you are waiting for the CD to mature, interest rates may rise, causing you to miss out on an opportunity to make a higher return. Interest rate risk is less of an issue with a short-term CD. A short-term CD is a good investment in periods when interest rates are expected to rise. By not being locked in for a long time period, you can catch the upswing of the interest rates by reinvesting the CD at maturity into another short-term CD with a higher rate. The opposite is true if interest rates were expected to fall over the coming years; you would rather have a longer-term CD to lock in the higher interest rate.

There are a few things to be aware of with CDs. Some are "callable," which means that the issuing institution can force you into redeeming the CD early and you lose out on potential returns. This usually happens when interest rates are falling. There are also penalties for early withdrawal. You need to get in writing how often they pay dividends, how often they compound the interest, the APY or Annual Percentage Yield, and when the maturity date is. Also, be aware that some CDs automatically roll over into another CD once the time period is up if you don't stop the rollover. If it does roll over before you catch it, you may be paying a penalty if you try to withdraw your money "early."

## SHORT-TERM BONDS

Bonds are really just loans. Governments and corporations need to raise money from time to time to build new roads or schools, create new factories, or build other big projects. In order to raise the money, they can issue bonds. Buying a bond is essentially you loaning money to a government or a corporation.

Bonds are like any other loan. If you take out a car loan from a bank, you agree to pay the principal amount plus a specified interest rate over a specified time period. So when you buy a bond, the corporation agrees to return your money with interest, called **the coupon**, over a specific time period, called the **time to maturity**. Bonds may pay the interest out once a year, once a quarter, or every month, but most generally it pays semi-annually. If you hold the bond to maturity, your money is returned in its entirety. The amount that the entity agrees to repay you at maturity is known as **face value** or **par value**. The interest rate is called the coupon rate. (The reason it's called the coupon rate is that before bonds were electronically traded, people would clip the coupon on the bond paperwork and take it to the bank to get the interest paid).

For example, Corporation ABC wants to build a new factory and decides to issue bonds to pay for that factory. You decide to purchase one of the bonds for $1,000, which pays 7% interest over five years. So you have a bond with a par value of $1,000 with a 7% coupon rate and a five-year maturity time frame. So each year you should receive $70 in interest payment and at the end of the five years you will get your $1,000 back.

Bonds can be bought and sold like stocks, so at any given moment the price of a bond can fluctuate just like that of a stock. Depending on the markets and interest rates, inflation, and so on, the price of the bond may be more or less than what you paid for it. So you own the above $1,000 bond with the coupon rate of 7% and time to maturity of five years. You have some bills due and need money to pay them and decide that you want to sell your bond. But the market has changed and a bond similar to the one you own can now be bought with an interest rate of 8%. In order for you to entice someone to buy your bond with a lower interest rate that produces less in interest payments than what they could currently get, you now have to sell the bond at a discount for, say, $750. But if you decide that you don't need the cash and instead decide to hold it to maturity, it doesn't matter that the price for a 7% coupon bond like yours is now trading at only $750, you will still get your full $1,000 back at maturity because that's the agreement you had with the corporation to which you loaned your money.

Bonds, like CDs, are subject to interest rate risk or the risk that the interest rates will rise while you own the bond. If interest rates rise, you may miss out on an opportunity to capitalize on a higher interest rate than what you currently own, or your bond may lose value, as in the discussion above. Bonds are also subject to credit risk. **Credit risk** is the risk you assume when lending money, via buying a bond, that the borrower will be unable to pay you back, or the risk of default on the loan. Companies are just like people and need to be investigated prior to lending them money. Would you rather loan $1,000 to someone with no job and a maxed-out credit card who agrees to pay you back with 15% interest, or would you prefer to loan $1,000 to someone with no debt and a steady job that he has held for the last 20 years at 6% interest? Your preference depends on whether or not you like to gamble.

**Short-term bonds** are those bonds or bond funds that hold bonds that mature in one-to-three years. **Ultra short-term bonds** mature in 180 days to 1.5 years and are useful in periods where interest rates are expected to rise, just like with shorter-term CDs. They provide some return on your money and can be relatively safe, depending on what you invest in (think person with no job vs. person with a steady job). There are also bond funds that will hold many different bonds. Be aware that some bond funds invest in less than stellar companies to make the funds look better by increasing the rate of return. This can be a big issue during periods of poor credit and collapse like we saw in 2008 as companies went under.

You may want to check out T-bills, also called Treasury bills, which are loans to the US Government. Historically, they have had less credit risk and can be tax-exempt. T-bills can be purchased directly from the US Government through www.treasurydirect.gov. T-bills are issued from the US Government for terms of up to one year. These have minimal credit risk and therefore carry low rates of return. T-bills are typically sold at a discount to par value (the amount they are worth at maturity) and redeemed at full par value at maturity. So you may buy the T-bill for $900 but get $1,000 back at maturity.

One question people have is why they should invest in short-term bonds when their interest rates are low? For example, the rates in 2015 were around 1%–2%. Why bother? If you keep all of your money in cash you can lose purchasing power to inflation. By investing in short-term bonds, you can usually make out slightly better than the inflation rate. Also, as interest rates rise, you will be able to catch the upswing with short-term bonds. However, it is usually a better bet to own a bond fund over an individual bond because the fund can get better prices when it buys bonds than an individual investor can get. This is because bond funds purchase large blocks of bonds direct from the seller.

One final comment about bonds: You are usually taxed at your normal income tax rate for corporate bonds and most bond funds. Both of these are best held in a tax-advantaged retirement account. Bonds issued from governments may be tax-free at the local, state, or federal level, or even all three. It just depends to whom you are loaning the money and what the tax laws are regarding that entity.

**TAKEAWAYS**

■ Savings accounts, money market deposit accounts, and short-term CDs are good places to hold money that you will need in the near future.

■ Do not confuse a money market deposit account with a money market mutual fund. The deposit account is like a savings account, and the mutual fund is just that, a mutual fund whose NAV is $1 and does not fluctuate.

■ Do not confuse APR and APY. APR is the percentage of interest you receive for the year. APY takes into account how often the interest is compounded. Use the APY to compare different opportunities.

■ If interest rates rise, bond prices will fall and vice versa.

■ Earnings from CDs, deposit accounts, and bonds are taxed at your normal income tax rate.

**TO-DO LIST**

☐ Determine the projected amount of money that you need for the next year or two. Remember that if you are working, you may only need a six-month rainy day fund, because you have a continuous inflow of cash from your job and a great disability policy. If you need to make a large purchase or have a risky job situation, then you will need to hold more in cash.

☐ Hold the money you need for the next year or two in a cash account, savings bond, CD, or other liquid account that will hold its value.

# CHAPTER 8

# YOU NEED THE MONEY IN THREE-TO-FIVE YEARS

This chapter will focus on investment types that are best suited for money that you won't need for at least the next three-to-five years. These investment vehicles normally have less risk and less return than those investments that are used for money that you won't need for at least three years or more. These intermediate-term investments include the following:

- Savings Bonds (Series EE/I)
- Longer-Term CDs
- Intermediate Bonds
- What to Check When Evaluating Bonds
- Types of Bonds

## SAVINGS BONDS (SERIES EE/I)

Savings bonds? Really? As an investment? Isn't that what grandparents give their grandchildren? Yep. They can be good, safe investments in the right setting. Savings bonds are short-term debt that the US Government issues to finance the running of the government. These are guaranteed by the full faith and credit of the US Government and considered ultra safe, as of the writing of this book. These can now only be purchased directly from the US Government through the website www.treasurydirect.gov.

Savings bonds come in several varieties. I will talk about the Series EE and I bonds. The **Series EE savings bond** is the most common of the savings bonds. It is now only issued in an electronic form, which you purchase for full face value. The interest rate for these bonds is based on the current interest rates. EE savings bonds produce dividends twice a year for up to 30 years. You can redeem them after five years with no penalty. If you redeem within one-to-five years, you lose the last three months of interest payments. These bonds can be redeemed at local banks. You can check the value of a particular savings bond at www.treasurydirect.gov. The EE bonds are best used with higher interest rates that are expected to start falling.

The **Series I savings bond** has an interest rate that is adjusted for inflation. The interest rate resets every six months. It carries a fixed rate plus a rate adjusted for the prevailing inflation rates. This is especially important if inflation and interest rates are expected to rise. Avoid these bonds if the fixed rate is at zero, as it has been recently, because you will be locked into that zero for up to 30 years. Also be aware that if inflation is negative, the overall interest rate of the I-bond can fall to zero, even if the fixed component is above zero.

Savings bonds are taxed federally at your normal rate but are exempt from state and local taxes. If you use these bonds for certain educational expenses, they may also be exempt from federal taxes. Check with your tax advisor or the government for the qualifying expenses.

## LONGER-TERM CDs

These are identical to the short-term CDs but carry higher interest rate risk. They can be purchased at a bank. They come in one-, two-, three-, five-, and ten-year issues. Pick the time period that correlates most closely to when you need the money. Be aware of interest rate risk, which increases as the length of the CD increases.

## INTERMEDIATE BONDS

As stated earlier, a bond is simply a loan to a government or a corporation to finance a particular activity. If it is the US Government, intermediate bonds will be called Treasury notes, or Treasury bonds, depending on the length of time to repayment (two-to-ten years, more than ten years, respectively). If corporations issue them, they are called corporate bonds. And if they are from state or local governments, they are called municipal bonds and are also known as tax-free munis because of tax treatment, which I will discuss later.

There are also zero-coupon bonds, which you should generally avoid. "Zero-coupon" means that you pay a reduced price for the bond, and at maturity the company will pay the full face value instead of paying periodic "coupon" payments, hence the name of the bond. So you might buy the zero-coupon bond for $750 and get $1,000 back at maturity. Sounds great that you have to pay less and get more, right? You need to be careful with these bonds, however, because you must pay tax on the phantom "interest" each year even though you don't receive it until maturity. This is especially important if the company is financially risky and has a chance of defaulting, because not only have you have been paying taxes on money you haven't received yet, but you may not get paid back at maturity if the company defaults. A double whammy.

You can purchase new bonds directly from the government, municipal governments, or corporations. Municipal bonds can be purchased through an investment house or discount broker, or you can get them directly from the municipality, depending on the amount you wish to purchase. Treasuries can be purchased directly from the government at www.treasury direct.gov. However, for most bonds, the easiest place to purchase them is through an investment house or discount broker, just like buying stocks.

Most new bonds are sold in "blocks" which are monetary and may be as large as $100,000 or even $1,000,000 for a block. It can be difficult for an individual investor to afford them, especially if you only wanted one or two bonds for $1,000 or $2,000. This is why they are usually purchased through an investment house or discount broker, which functions as the middleman. But, because you are purchasing through a middleman, you usually don't get great prices because you are paying a **spread**. The spread is the difference between the price at which the broker buys the bond and the price he sells it to you. You may also have to pay transaction fees. Be aware that many sellers will not tell you what the fees are. Some bond sellers like Fidelity are fairly transparent and will list their fees but not the spreads.

You can also purchase bond funds. Going with a broad-based bond fund is usually a wiser idea. That's because not only can the bond fund get significantly better prices than you can due to their buying directly from the bond issuer but the fund will be more diversified than you will be by owning one individual bond.

## WHAT TO CHECK WHEN EVALUATING BONDS

When you consider purchasing a bond, there are several parameters you should check out in order to compare apples to apples and know what you are buying. This section briefly discusses coupon rate, yield to maturity, callable vs. non-callable, credit rating, and risks.

### COUPON

The coupon, as we discussed earlier, is the amount of the interest that the borrower agrees to pay per year.

### YIELD TO MATURITY

**Yield to Maturity (YTM)** is the total percentage you receive if the bond is held to maturity and is more important than the coupon rate when comparing similar bonds. This takes into account the price that you pay for the bond, as well as the coupon rate. So if the coupon rate is 5% on a $100 bond and you paid the full $100 for it, then the YTM is 5%. But if you buy the bond at a discount of $95, the YTM then becomes 5.2%, because it takes into account the $5 in capital gains, in addition to the yearly distributions, when you are paid $100 back at maturity. This is particularly important if you are evaluating bonds trading at a **premium** (more than face value) or at a **discount** (less than face value). As stated earlier, you will pay tax on both the distributions and the capital gains at your normal tax rate.

### CALLABLE VS. NON-CALLABLE

If you own a **callable bond**, the issuing institution could "call the bond" and decide to repay you earlier than the agreed-upon maturity date. A **non-callable** bond means that the borrower cannot repay the bond until the stated maturity. Your bond is subject to **call risk** if it is a callable bond. Call risk means that if the borrowing institution calls the bond, you lose out on future interest payments. It may seem great for you to get your money back early. But usually if the borrower is calling the bond it is because they can get a new "loan" cheaper because interest rates have fallen. This means that when you go to reinvest, you will get a lower interest rate than you had previously. To make up for the call risk, callable bonds usually come with a higher coupon rate.

## CREDIT RATING

**Credit Risk** is the risk that an issuer of a bond (company or government) will default and not pay you back your money. Standard and Poor's (S&P) and Moody's rates issuers via **credit ratings**. The best ratings are "investment-grade" bonds, which include AAA through BBB for S&P ratings. These ratings suggest that the bonds have little risk of default and tend to have lower yields. "Junk bond" ratings include BB and lower for S&P. These will have a higher risk of default but usually carry higher yields to offset the risk of default.

One note is needed here. Be careful of what you are buying. Good ratings do not always mean that you are getting high-quality, low-risk bonds. If a bond is insured by an insurance company, the credit rating is based on the insurance company's rating even if the bond is a junk bond. This means that a junk bond could show up with a AAA rating. So be aware of what you are buying.

| BOND CREDIT RATINGS | | |
| --- | --- | --- |
| GRADE | MOODY's RATING | S&P RATING |
| Investment | Aaa | AAA |
| Investment | Aa | AA |
| Investment | A | A |
| Investment | Baa | BBB |
| High-Yield | Ba | BB |
| High-Yield | B | B |
| High-Yield | Caa | CCC |
| High-Yield | Ca | CC/C |
| High-Yield | C | D |

## RISKS

Several types of risks are inherent to bonds: interest rate risk, credit risk, reinvestment risk, and inflation risk.

**Interest rate risk**, as we discussed earlier, is the risk that the interest rates will rise during the period that you own the bond. This will make the bond you are holding worth less if you chose to sell it prior to maturity because investors can go buy a similar bond with a higher interest rate. This does not matter if you hold it to maturity. The closer it gets to maturity, the closer the value of the bond gets to par value. Bond prices and interest rates tend to move in opposite directions because of the interest rate risk. Bonds are a good option if you are in a high interest rate environment/ hot economy that is expected to cool off and interest rates are expected to start falling. The opposite is true if interest rates are expected to rise. You don't want to be holding a ten-year bond that will become much less valuable if interest rates are rising.

For example, prior to the recession of 2007–2008, bond interest rates were doing well with the Fed funds rate (rate at which banks lend money to each other overnight) over 5%. During the recession, the Federal Reserve had a monetary easing policy that drove interest rates low, causing bond prices to go up. The prices went up because the "older" bonds had higher interest rates than you could get by buying "new" bonds. When the Fed begins to raise interest rates again, the opposite will be true and you would expect bond prices to begin to fall. Not a great time to purchase intermediate or long-term bonds. It would be probably a better time to buy short-term bonds so you can catch rising interest rates. Expected future interest rates become important if you are invested in a bond fund. Bond funds are more susceptible to bond price movement, as funds do not generally hold the bonds to maturity.

Bonds can be vulnerable to **credit risk** if interest rates are rising rapidly. This is especially true if the issuing institution is less than stellar financially. If the institution has to take on more debt and is unable to handle paying the higher interest rates, it may end up defaulting on your bond.

**Reinvestment risk** is the risk that interest rates fall while you are holding a bond. Once the bond matures, you are stuck reinvesting into a bond with a lower interest rate than the one you had.

**Inflation risk** is present with all investment choices. It happens if you are holding an investment with a return that is less than the current inflation rate. If you are making 2% returns and inflation is 3%, you are actually losing money to inflation. This happens commonly if you are holding cash or other low interest rate investments like bonds since 2000.

| MOVEMENT OF BONDS AND RISKS WITH REGARDS TO INTEREST RATES | | | |
|---|---|---|---|
| | INTEREST RATE ↑ | INTEREST RATE ↓ | Comments |
| **BOND PRICE** | ↓ | ↑ | When interest rates rise, bonds sell at a discount to be competitive with new bonds with higher interest rates |
| **RISK** | Reinvestment & Credit Risks | Bond gets called | When interest rates rise, bond holders may miss out on better interest rates; When interest rates fall, bond may get called |
| **BEST BOND TO HOLD** | Short-term Bond Fund | Intermediate Bond Fund | Short-term bond allows quick reinvestment to catch rising rates; long-term bond captures a higher rate if interest rates falling |

## TYPES OF BONDS

When you are considering buying bonds, you will find many types of bonds and bond funds to choose from. They include bonds issued by the US Government, municipal governments, and corporations.

### US GOVERNMENT SECURITIES/TREASURIES

These are issued by the US Government and come as T-bills (Treasury bills), Treasury notes, and Treasury bonds, depending on maturity length. T-bills mature in less than 12 months, Treasury notes in two-to-ten years, and Treasury bonds in more than ten years. Many come with tax breaks and carry a slightly lower return because of those tax breaks and low credit risk. They do not have significant credit risk because the US Government has the ability to tax and print money. The chance of default is close to zero. The longer the bond maturity, the more volatility in price will be expected over the long term due to interest rate and inflation risk, giving rise to higher yields. You can purchase these from the website www.treasurydirect.gov.

| U.S. GOVERNMENT SECURITIES MATURITIES | |
| --- | --- |
| **T-BILLS** . . . . . . . . . . . . . . . . . | Less than 12 months |
| **TREASURY NOTES**. . . . . . . . . | 2–10 years |
| **TREASURY BONDS** . . . . . . . . | More than 10 years |

## TAX-FREE MUNICIPAL BONDS (MUNIS)

State and municipal governments raise money for state and city government projects through **municipal bonds**. There are two types: General Obligation and Revenue bonds. General Obligation bonds are used to pay for non-toll roads and schools, and are guaranteed to be paid back. Revenue bonds, which are used to pay for special projects like toll roads, are paid back through revenue produced from the project, but there is no guarantee that they will be paid back. Municipal bonds are tax-exempt from federal income taxes, which makes them of interest to high-income earners in the highest tax brackets. You can purchase these from the governments themselves or through online brokers. If you use a broker, the bond price will have a markup. The only way to avoid the markup is to purchase directly from the governments, but you may have to pony up $100,000 or more.

## CORPORATE BONDS

Corporate bonds allow companies to finance activities such as building new factories. These bonds are subjected to credit risk, more so than government bonds, since corporations do not have a taxing authority to pay back the bonds. So if you are going to own only one corporate bond, before you buy that bond, you need to make sure that the company is not going to default.

## JUNK BONDS/HIGH-YIELD BONDS

**High-yield bonds** refer to bonds from companies or governments with poor credit ratings. These are below investment grade, with ratings of BB/Ba or lower. These bonds carry high yields (hence their name) to compensate for the greater possibility of default. **Junk bonds** refer to the bottom tiers of the high-yield bonds, although some use the terms interchangeably. Most of these are very volatile and belong in a portfolio only as a speculative component.

## BOND FUNDS

Bond funds are like stock mutual funds but are made up of a collection of individual bonds. You cannot rely on the name of the fund to know what is in the fund, so you must evaluate the prospectus. They can slip in high-yield bonds to increase the yield rates. Bond funds don't typically hold bonds to maturity, so there can be significant changes in fund value as the price of the bonds and interest rates fluctuate.

When looking for a bond fund, make sure the fees are low, just like with stock funds. A total bond market index fund is a great choice as it provides good diversity to your bond portfolio. These types of index funds carry low fees. You should know the bond fund's credit risk. Just like stocks, a low-fee, broad-based bond fund with a good mix of corporate and government bonds and even with some high-yield funds will do the best. That way you can capitalize on market movements. Just like with individual bonds, longer-term bonds in the fund will significantly increase volatility and risk. You should understand that if the interest rates are at historic lows, you should consider a broad-based short-term bond fund to be ready to catch the rising interest rates, and if the interest rates are at historic highs, consider an intermediate-term broad-based bond fund because the rates will most likely fall, although that is not guaranteed. But always remember to find those funds that have low fees and expenses. If you are concerned about market timing and figuring out what interest rates are doing, stick to short-term bond funds unless interest rates are at historic highs.

## TAKEAWAYS

- If interest rates are expected to rise in the near future, ultra short-term bonds, savings bonds adjusted for inflation, and CDs are a better investment strategy that will allow you to catch the upswing in interest rates.
- Be aware of credit risk and interest rate risk when investing in bonds.
- If you are in one of the highest tax brackets, consider tax-exempt municipal bonds.
- Evaluate different bond options by comparing the yield to maturity (YTM), as this takes into account the compounding of the dividends and the current price of the bond. You can also compare new issue bonds based on the Annual Percentage Yield (APY), which takes the compounding of dividends into account since the price being paid is the par value.

## TO-DO LIST

- ☐ Determine how much money you need for the next three-to-five years. Keep in mind that if you are still working and are not near retirement, you may not need to hold as much money in these investments because you have a continuous flow of cash from your job and may be able to keep more in long-term investments like stocks. If you are nearing retirement, make sure you have the necessary funds invested in these mid-range accounts to protect your retirement from problems that crop up with stock market fluctuations.

- ☐ Make sure to compare apples to apples by looking at the APY, credit ratings, and so on of the investment choices.

# CHAPTER 9

# YOU NEED THE MONEY IN MORE THAN FIVE YEARS

The investments discussed in this chapter tend to be more volatile and less predictable in the short term. But they tend to have better returns on investments over the long term and are most appropriate for money that you will not need for at least five years. This chapter will look at the following investments:

- Intermediate Bonds
- Stocks
- Reading Investment Prospectuses and Looking at the Numbers
- Master Limited Partnerships (MLP)
- Real Estate and REITS (Real Estate Investment Trusts)
- Gold

## INTERMEDIATE BONDS

If you need the money in more than five years, you can consider an intermediate bond fund. Intermediate bonds are of use if bond yields are high, and interest rates are expected to fall. Consider an intermediate-length bond fund (three to 15 years as a ballpark figure) so you can lock in those higher interest rates for a longer period. Intermediate bonds also come with higher yields than short-term bonds. Funds to consider include an index fund made up of intermediate-length (15-year) corporate bonds with a lower, but still investment-grade, rating. An alternative to consider if you are in one of the highest tax brackets is a tax-free muni index fund.

You need to know where the interest rates are and take an educated guess as to what the markets are doing. You don't want to be locked into a low interest rate, 15-year bond if the interest rates are expected to rise.

If you are choosing intermediate-length bonds, the reason you pick lower but still investment-grade bonds is that they have a lower default risk than non-investment-grade junk bonds. And because they don't have perfect credit ratings, they come with higher yields than high investment-grade bonds (like AAA). If you choose long-term bonds (20–30 years), they have much higher volatility compared with the yield they produce. That means that they have much more risk to reward than the intermediate-term ones because the likelihood of the interest rates changing over the 20–30 years is very high. So experts say the sweet spot for intermediate-term bonds tends to be buying A- or BBB-rated, 15-year bonds.

## STOCKS

Over the long term, stocks have been one of the best-performing asset classes, going by past performance. Many experts recommend using the broadest market index fund you can find for diversification, keeping costs low, and then leaving the money alone in your account for at least five years, only doing the occasional rebalancing. As stated earlier, you still must rebalance your accounts at least once a year, if not more often.

When you buy a stock, you are purchasing shares of ownership in a company. These are sold on exchanges, and the amount of demand for the stock causes the price to fluctuate. In addition, the price of the stock reflects the underlying business health, investor sentiment, the level of expected and previous dividends, and the amount of expected growth. There are different types of stock shares that are available. You can buy common stock shares or preferred stock shares. The ones most commonly traded through your brokerage accounts is common stock.

**Common stock** is stock ownership that comes with voting rights in the company. You can vote management in or out but have no control over day-to-day operations. The down side is if the business fails, the common stock shareholders will be the last to get their money back, if at all. If the company has financial issues during the year, dividend distributions may get cut. Shares of common stock produce gains through both stock price appreciation and through dividends.

Stocks return profits to shareholders through **dividends**, which usually come out on a quarterly basis. Not all companies will produce dividends. A small, rapidly expanding company may plow the proceeds back into the company to grow the business and thus produce no dividends. Think of an early start-up Facebook or Tesla. People who buy these stocks are looking for a company's stock price to skyrocket rather than counting on income from dividends.

Some investors are looking for steady income by way of dividends instead of stock price appreciation. Companies with higher, more consistent dividends will tend to be the large, older companies that do not have a need for quick growth. They spin off more of the profits as dividends. Think IBM or Exxon Mobile.

**Preferred stock** tends to be a hybrid between common stock and bonds. The stockholder is usually guaranteed a fixed dividend. The preferred stock dividends can be significantly higher than those for common stock and are distributed before common stockholders' dividends. In return, preferred stockholders usually get no voting rights. But if the company goes into bankruptcy, preferred shares will get prioritized, after the bondholders but before the common stockholders, to get their money back. Those purchasing preferred stock shares are looking for larger and more consistent dividends than for stock price appreciation, which tends to be much less than for common stock.

Preferred stock is similar to a bond in that there is a guaranteed dividend paid semi-annually or quarterly at a specified interest rate. People and institutions may invest in these for an income stream. But unless you are a company that gets special tax breaks, the dividends are generally taxed at your ordinary income tax rate, like bonds. However, some preferred stock dividends may qualify for the capital gains rate.

| COMMON STOCK vs. PREFERRED STOCK | |
|---|---|
| COMMON | Buy for price appreciation; some dividends; last to be paid back in bankruptcy |
| PREFERRED | Higher, consistent dividends; less price appreciation, hybrid between common stock and a bond; has par value; paid back before common stockholders in bankruptcy |

With preferred stock, many "issues" (the shares) sell for $25, which is their par value. Like bonds, these can be callable, which means that the company can redeem them early anytime after the callable date. When they are redeemed, they are generally redeemed for par value, which is usually $25. These stocks trade on exchanges and move up and down in price, but much less so than common stock does. If you buy the preferred stock when it is trading at $26 and shortly thereafter it gets called, you lose money, because it will be called for the par value of $25. Try to buy these stocks at or less than par value. These stocks also have interest rate risk and credit risk like bonds. www.preferredstockchannel.com/ is a good place to find information on the stock's callable date and par value as well as the dividend tax rate and current trading price.

## TYPES OF COMPANIES

Companies are usually lumped into categories such as small caps or large caps, growth stocks or values stocks, international stocks, energy stocks, healthcare stocks, cyclicals, and so on. Each category has certain characteristics that lend the stocks in them to be good investments at different points in the economic cycle or depending on your investment strategies. I am discussing these so you know what the terms mean in case your advisor, friend, family, or acquaintance mentions these.

### SMALL CAP

Small cap is short for small capitalization, which describes how much the companies are worth, generally $1 billion or less. Small cap stocks are small companies that have a lot of potential for growth, but whose stocks can be volatile and risky. They tend to pay fewer dividends, because the money goes back into the company to stimulate growth. The upside can be quicker stock price appreciation. These stocks are like young entrepreneurs. They tend to take more risks than your typical 50-year-old but could very well become the next billionaire.

## LARGE CAP

Large caps are very large, generally older, more stable companies with a market capitalization over $10 billion. As behemoths, they have a difficult time growing. They return more of the profits back to the shareholders as dividends instead of reinvesting them to stimulate more growth. These companies are less risky and less prone to stock price volatility. These are the General Electrics and IBMs of the world. They are more stable in financial turmoil (when the stock market is rapidly fluctuating) than the small caps.

## MID CAP

In between $1 billion and $10 billion market capitalization are the mid cap companies. They are in between the small caps and the large caps with a mix of growth and dividends.

The small, mid, and large cap companies are based on size and market valuation. Companies can also be grouped according to growth vs. value, where they are located (US vs. Non-US, Pacific Rim, etc.), or what they produce (healthcare, financials, energy, consumer staples, etc.).

| COMPANY SIZE CHARACTERISTICS | |
|---|---|
| **SMALL CAP:** | < $1 Billion, ↑ growth, ↓ dividends |
| **MID CAP:** | $1–10 billion |
| **LARGE CAP:** | > $10 billion, ↓ growth, ↑ dividends |

## GROWTH STOCKS

Companies that are **growth stocks** tend to be smaller and have a higher expected growth rate and stock price appreciation, although they aren't always small companies. They tend to be exciting stocks like Tesla and Twitter. Investors pay for the possibilities of large jumps in stock prices. These companies may have little to no dividends because they plow the money back into the company to accelerate growth.

## VALUE STOCKS

**Value stocks** are stocks of companies whose prices have been hammered down for particular reasons or whose stock is simply underappreciated. Value stocks tend to be good companies, but something bad has happened to them or they may be in a boring sector and forgotten about. For example, a toy company has a great financial statement and has done well in the past but recently had an issue with a toy recall. The stock price gets hammered down. The company corrects the cause of the recall, but the stock price still remains low. Investors who hunt for value stocks will see this stock and realize that the price is discounted from what it should be. They then buy the stock and wait for the price to rebound back to the level it should actually be trading at. These stocks tend to be less volatile in a volatile market because they have already been hammered down and don't fall as hard and fast as growth stocks in a recession. Buying value stocks is like going to a yard sale for stocks. You can get great stocks at discount prices. Warren Buffet is famous for investing in this type of stock.

| GROWTH vs. VALUE STOCKS | |
|---|---|
| **GROWTH**: | Investor looking for fast rise in stock price; not looking for large dividends |
| **VALUE**: | Price has been beaten down, stock is "on sale;" better in financial turmoil |

## INTERNATIONAL STOCKS

**International stocks** are typically more volatile than US stocks. International stock funds generally have higher management fees than the US stock funds because they require more oversight. This is especially true in emerging markets where there can be political unrest, currency issues, corruption, and so on. International funds can include **all world**, which hold both US and non-US stocks; **emerging markets**, which are the fast growing "new" markets like India and Brazil; **European markets**; **Non-US**; and any combination thereof. You need to know that if you are holding a broad-based US stock market fund, you already have about 30% international exposure through US companies doing business abroad. If you feel the need for more, the general advice from most investment pros is to keep international stocks under 10% of your portfolio to limit the risk involved in these markets, because they can be quite volatile.

## CYCLICAL and NON-CYCLICAL STOCKS and SECTORS

Stocks can be classified as **cyclical stocks** or **non-cyclical stocks**. They really should be renamed "Non-necessary" (cyclical) and "Necessary" (non-cyclical) stocks. **Non-necessary/Cyclical stocks** include stocks that sell discretionary items like cars, high-end watches, and building materials like steel. These prices are likely to fall in a recession and rise in recovery; hence the cyclical nature. **Necessary/Non-cyclical stocks**, also known as defensive stocks, include companies that sell necessities like bleach, toothpaste, and staple food items like bread. These are also known as consumer staples. People will always buy these products, even in a recession. If there is a downturn in the market, investors rush to these stocks because they won't lose as much value as the non-necessary stocks.

The terms cyclical and non-cyclical relate to economy upswings and downswings. When the economy is in a recession, the non-cyclical, necessary stocks, including defensive/consumer staples, do better. Why? Because food and essential items are usually the only things consumers are purchasing. If people are worried about losing their homes or their jobs, they are not likely to go buy a car or build a new home.

As the economy recovers, businesses and consumers will begin spending on more discretionary items (the cyclical, non-necessary stocks). Companies will invest in new factories and people will build new homes; the companies that manufacture steel and building supplies will prosper. Companies that make luxury items such as high-end clothes, jewelry, and cars will also do well. These stocks are considered cyclical because they will rise and fall with the economic cycle.

Different sectors will rise and fall during the economic cycle. **Sectors** include consumer goods broken down into discretionary and staples, energy, healthcare, basic materials, financials, industrials, technology, utilities, and telecommunications. The basic sectors are a bit subjective depending on who you ask. But in general, these are the ones you will hear and read about. Economic cycles include expansion and contraction of the economy. So investors who trade stocks based on the economic cycle will look for the best performer in a particular sector that is expected to take off, based on where they think the economy is in its cycle. If they think that the economy is headed into a recession, they start buying consumer staple stocks. Smart investors are buying these as everyone else is selling them because the prices are falling to new lows. And vice versa. If the economy is headed toward recovery, you start buying technology and materials stocks. The idea is to buy at the bottom when stock prices in those sectors are at their lowest so that as the sector recovers you can catch the appreciation of the stock values.

| CYCLICAL vs. NON-CYCLICAL STOCKS | |
|---|---|
| **CYCLICAL (Non-necessity):** | Good in booming economy; includes discretionary items (luxury goods and cars), materials like steel to build homes, and financials |
| **NON-CYCLICAL (Necessity):** | Better in economic downturn; includes consumer staples (like food and toothpaste), utilities, and healthcare |

# READING INVESTMENT PROSPECTUSES AND LOOKING AT THE NUMBERS

We will be discussing how to read and evaluate financial statements in part III: "FINANCIAL STATEMENTS." Reading a financial statement for your practice is the same as for a publicly traded company. The same rules apply to prospectuses and company financials as apply to your own practice financials, except that with public companies, you have to be sure to read the fine print. The notes and addendums usually tell you any issues the company is having. They have to legally notify the investor, so of course they bury it in the fine print. If you are going to own an individual stock or bond, or a mutual fund, you must look at the prospectus and make sure it is something that you think will be profitable. If you don't feel like putting in the time, then just purchase a broad-based index fund.

# MASTER LIMITED PARTNERSHIPS (MLP)

**MLP** investments combine a partnership with the liquidity of a company that is publicly traded. These partnerships involve real estate, commodities, or natural resources. This is because, by law, 90% of their revenue must be from one of these three sources. An example of this is ownership in an oil pipeline, where the MLP charges a "toll" for allowing the oil to be transported through the pipeline.

An MLP is taxed under a business structure that allows a large percentage of the income to pass through to the "limited partner." Due to this structure, the MLP makes money and passes your portion of the profits on to you before some expenses, write-offs, and depreciation are subtracted out. Because of that income pass-through, MLPs can generate large distributions. The majority of the distribution is offset by your share of the write-offs and depreciation and is not taxed. (See "FINANCIAL LITERACY: DEPRECIATION/AMORTIZATION" in chapter 12 for a discussion of why depreciation affects the paper value of income but not the actual account value.) Only a small part of your distribution is actually seen and taxed as income. However, this income is taxed at your normal tax rate.

The portion of your distributions that is not recorded as income is seen as the return of your investment. This decreases your cost basis. **Cost basis** is loosely the amount that you invested. (Your accountant will rightfully argue that there is a lot more that goes into figuring out the actual cost basis of your investment.) A decrease in your cost basis means that the value of your initial investment has decreased. It's confusing, so let's look at an example.

Let's say that you pay $10,000 for the initial MLP investment, and in the first year you receive $2,500 in distributions. Of that amount, $500 is considered income, which is taxed at your normal income rate, and the other $2,000 was offset by depreciation expense, write-offs, and so on. That $2,000 is not taxed and is treated as **return of capital** (initial investment), which lowers your cost basis. So your $10,000 investment now appears with $8,000 as its book value.

Okay, so what's the issue? The issue is that when you go to sell the MLP, you will have to pay tax on the gains. At the end of five years your cost basis is $0 (you were paid back tax-deferred $2,000/year), you sell it for the same $10,000 that you initially bought it for (no real capital appreciation). But you have to pay tax on the entire $10,000 because now your cost basis is $0 with $10,000 in gains. Essentially, the tax breaks that you received over the last five years just came due.

Why should you buy an MLP then? Because this can be a useful strategy to tax-defer your payments until you are in a lower tax bracket. Also, because your tax basis (money invested) cannot go below zero, these make sense if you plan on holding them for a very long time to take advantage of the tax savings. The tax bill will come due later, including part capital gains rates and part normal income tax rates. If MPLs are willed to the next generation, you will avoid taxation via estate tax laws.

Okay, you say, "What about holding it in my retirement account so I don't have to deal with tax issues." Not so fast. If you hold it in there, you will be losing out on some of the tax benefits that MLPs provide such as the tax deferment. Also, if the income from the MLP goes over $1,000, you'll have to pay tax on it anyway. Keep it out of your retirement account.

The taxes for an MLP are complex and involve special forms. Limited partnerships create K-1s, which complicate your tax return and aren't always received before April 15, causing you to need a tax deadline extension. If your MLP income portion rises over a certain threshold and it does business in numerous states (like a pipeline crossing several states), you may have to file and pay tax in multiple states. You must be aware of the tax laws in all of the states that the MLP operates in. MLPs can be fraught with tax issues and should be discussed with your tax advisor before purchasing. You need to fully understand how the MLP will affect your tax burden.

## REAL ESTATE AND REITS (REAL ESTATE INVESTMENT TRUSTS)

Real estate can be a great asset to own due to beneficial tax treatment. But because there are so many books on real estate investing and because the topic is very broad, I will only discuss REITS in this book, because they are traded similarly to stocks. Short of owning a ranch or an apartment building, owning a REIT is a great way to invest in real estate and get access to its poor asset correlation for your portfolio.

**REITS** are companies that buy, sell, and manage real estate or mortgages. There are two main types: equity or mortgage. A REIT can be generalist, holding a wide array of properties, or it can hold very specific types of properties like hospitals or shopping malls, or properties in certain parts of the country. There are also commercial or residential mortgage REITS. These investments can be private placement or publicly traded on the stock market. If not publicly traded, they can be purchased through a financial advisor or stockbroker but with high sales fees. The private REITS are very illiquid. Stick to the publicly traded, broad-based REITS with low fees, just like stocks.

REITS have poor asset correlation to most other assets, including stocks, and because of that, they can help mitigate risk in your portfolio. Equity REITS make money by buying properties and renting them out. Investors make money through the rents and property appreciation. They tend to be very stable long-term investments.

Mortgage REITS are **highly leveraged**, meaning that a significant portion of the money invested comes from borrowing rather than from money actually owned by the REIT, which makes them very risky. They make money by borrowing money at a lower short-term interest rate and using it to purchase higher long-term interest rate mortgages. The proceeds they make are based off of the spread. Mortgage REITS do not do well in periods of increasing interest rates. They can be very volatile. The mortgage REITs should probably be invested in only in a speculative account.

Because of the law, 90% of the income has to be passed on to REIT investors. This can mean large distributions, but it also means that the distributions you receive are taxed at your ordinary income tax rate. It is recommended that REITs be held within a retirement account that is tax-deferred to avoid the high taxes. REITs should be discussed with your tax professional, and you should understand how they would affect your taxes before purchasing them.

Once again, if you are using real estate to diversify your portfolio, holding a low-fee, index REIT ETF is probably the best way to go. As stated earlier, the goal is to diversify while keeping costs low. If you have several different irons in the fire at one time, you can hopefully catch the upswing in whichever asset class it is moving. You rebalance periodically and get ready for the next asset class to move.

## GOLD

Most people incorrectly believe that gold is a hedge against inflation. But studies have shown that there is really no correlation. Actually it appears that gold rises when interest rates fall, like they did in the 2008 recession when people panicked. So don't buy gold for its inflationary protection. Buy it because you want to further diversify your portfolio. Or buy it because you like the look and feel of gold jewelry. Or buy gold bars if you think the world will fall apart—they're easier to trade. But don't buy it because you think it will help protect against inflation. By the way, gold is regarded as a "collectible" (like stamps and artwork) by the US Government and is subject to a 28% tax rate instead of the normal 15%–20% capital gains rate. So it should only be held in a retirement account. The best way to hold gold, if you must hold it, is as part of a broad-based commodities fund with the sole purpose of increasing the diversity of your portfolio, because commodities tend to have negative correlation to other classes of assets.

## TAKEAWAYS

- If you are using bonds as an income generator, the sweet spot is considered to be lower-rated, investment-grade bonds of 15-years duration.
- Common stock has "earnings" from both stock price appreciation and dividend distributions. Plan on holding stocks for at least five years or more to limit the risk of having negative returns.
- Preferred stock is a hybrid between a bond and common stock with minimal price appreciation and a larger fixed dividend than common stock. Make sure to buy at or less than par value.
- A broad-based REIT can add diversification to your portfolio and tends to have poor correlation with other asset classes.
- Gold is not a hedge against inflation. If you must own gold, own it only to increase diversification of your portfolio via a broad commodities fund.

## TO-DO LIST

- ☐ Recheck the amount you have determined you need in the short and intermediate terms and invest the rest in the investments discussed in this chapter, namely stocks.

- ☐ Recheck which investments you have in your tax-advantaged retirement and non-tax-advantaged investment accounts to make sure that you have investments that are taxed at your normal tax rate in the retirement accounts.

- ☐ When in doubt as to what to invest in, go with a low-fee, broad-based index stock fund.

# CHAPTER 10

# IF YOU NEVER NEED THE MONEY: SPECULATION ACCOUNTS

The items in this chapter will be discussed in very general terms only, because they are very risky and beyond the scope of this book. They are actually **derivatives**, which provide control of an asset but no actual ownership of the underlying asset. They are highly leveraged and not recommended for retirement investing. They are being discussed here only to provide you with basic knowledge in case your financial advisor recommends them to you. This chapter will look at the following topics:

- Options
- Commodities and Futures
- Forex (Foreign Exchange)
- Las Vegas

If you decide to speculate in these derivatives, make sure you fully understand them prior to dabbling and use only money that you will never need. Make sure it is only a small percentage of your money and never part of your investment portfolio or retirement accounts. You need to understand that most of the derivatives discussed here are really just ophisticated forms of gambling. Do not confuse them with investments. Most of these are highly leveraged, meaning that with $1, you can control $10, $100, or even $1000 worth of "assets," which allow them to make quick incredible gains, but then also just as quickly lose a vast amount of money.

## OPTIONS

Options are derivatives of trading stocks. By buying one option, you are able to control 100 shares of stock. For example, if you expect the stock price to go up, you buy a **call option**. It gives you the right, but not an obligation, to buy 100 shares at a certain price (the strike price) before a certain time. If the price goes up, you "exercise your option" (which is presumably at a lower price than the stock is now trading) and take ownership of the stock. You can either take actual ownership of the stock, or more often than not, turn around and sell it at the current price and pocket the difference. You must be prepared to pony up the money for 100 shares of stock. And if that is for a "Google," it could cost you $90,000!

You can buy a **put option**, which means you have the option, but not the obligation, to sell shares to someone at a certain price by a particular time. You are betting that the stock price is going to fall. If the price does fall, you can "exercise your option" to sell the stock to some other investor and force them to pay a higher price than what the stock is actually trading at.

You can also sell a call or a put instead of buying them; and in doing so, you can collect a small amount money for "selling," even if you don't own the stock. This can be much more risky and can be considered "naked" if you don't own the underlying stock—BAD idea. This means that you may be required to deliver stock to someone and be forced to buy it at the current market price. You can lose a significant amount of money that way.

## COMMODITIES AND FUTURES

Commodities trading started as a way for farmers to sell their products. Some believe it began in 6000 B.C. in China as a way to trade rice. It provided a way for farmers to sell their crops before they were harvested, so they could lock in prices and protect themselves from the impact of weather on those crops. Commodities fall into four groups: metals, agricultural, livestock, and energy. Gold is a commodity. But, it is more often traded in the form of stocks of the gold mining companies than as the actual metal commodity. It is assumed that all commodities are the same regardless of where you buy them; for example, corn will be similar regardless of which farmer you buy it from. Commodities are traded through futures contracts, which are highly leveraged and can be very volatile. Two types of investors trade single commodities: the speculator and the hedger.

The **hedgers** are farmers or companies that buy futures contracts to hedge their risk of something happening to their product before they can sell it. For example, farmers enter into a futures contract to sell their crops in order to insulate themselves from natural disasters that may affect their crops. Or, an airline may purchase oil futures to hedge against future price increases of oil to better manage their company's risks of an increase in future fuel prices. If you are a farmer with crops to sell or a company that needs to mitigate risk, then by all means, trade commodities. Otherwise, you would be wise to avoid these. Don't be the **speculator** who is betting on the commodity price moving. If you are convinced that you need commodities because they tend to have negative correlation to the other asset classes, then hold a small amount of them in a broad based commodities fund. Don't hold just one type of commodity.

## FOREX (FOREIGN EXCHANGE)

**Forex (Foreign exchange)** is the buying and selling of currencies and is highly leveraged. It is usually leveraged at 50:1 or more. This means that if you put in $1,000, you can control up to $50,000. It always involves two currencies, and the exchange rates between the two. Because foreign exchange trading is so highly leveraged, investments can make tremendous profits or head south very quickly. This market is very liquid and trades 24 hours a day.

Exchange rates are listed as a pair of currencies. The first of the pair is what you are buying and the second is how much you are paying for it. For example, 1.20 EUR/USD means that you are buying one Euro and are paying pay $1.20 US for that Euro. There are two markets you can trade in, the spot market and the futures market. This futures market is different than the futures market for commodities.

The spot market occurs when you purchase the currency, like exchanging your $US for Euros at an exchange in a foreign country. The price and transfer of the physical property occurs immediately. In a futures market, the exchange rate is determined at the time of sale, but the transfer of the physical property occurs sometime in the future. These are fast-moving markets that can be very risky due to the amount of leverage. Even a move that is less than one cent can become a large amount because of leverage.

## LAS VEGAS

If you're speculating and gambling with your money anyway, you might as well go to Las Vegas and put some money on black. Or maybe play craps or blackjack, which have some of the best odds in the house and probably better odds than the aforementioned securities. If you lose money, at least hopefully you can say you had a nice vacation.

### TAKEAWAYS

- Only invest money in your speculation account that you never need.
- Commodities, options, and foreign exchange are highly leveraged and hence very risky investments.
- Do not confuse gold stocks of the mining companies with gold commodities.

### TO-DO LIST

- ☐ Avoid speculation.
- ☐ Repeat after me, "I will avoid speculation."

# PART III

## FINANCIAL STATEMENTS

Part III is meant to be an introduction to evaluating financial statements. It is presented only as a very brief overview of the basics, not as a course in accounting. The goal is to provide you with a base to build on as you become more comfortable looking at the numbers. Part III will cover only the most common items and discuss the most common ways you will see financial statements produced. Also, "practice," "business," and "company" will be used interchangeably.

# CHAPTER 11

# FINANCIAL STATEMENT BASICS

M any practices are multimillion-dollar companies. In the business world you would never find a CEO, CFO, president, or board member running a multimillion-dollar company with little to no financial knowledge. So why do we delude ourselves into thinking that is okay for us to run practices while lacking the ability to read and fully understand a financial statement? You need to take control, even if you have a practice manager who you think is "running" things. You must understand the elements of a complete financial statement and how you can use that statement to gauge how your practice is doing in relation to similar businesses. This chapter will look at the following topics:

- What is a Complete Financial Statement?
- Benchmarking
- Financial Literacy: Cash-Basis vs. Accrual Accounting
- Financial Literacy: Current vs. Long-Term

## WHAT IS A COMPLETE FINANCIAL STATEMENT?

Generally you need three reports to have complete financial statement: the **balance sheet**, the **income statement**, and the **statement of cash flow**. You should have at least two complete financial statements, one from the current year/period and one from the previous year/period in order to compare them to see the direction in which your practice or investment is going. If you only have the current period, you cannot see which way the numbers are trending, which is probably more important than the numbers themselves.

These three statements together tell you the health of the company or investment. They allow you to quickly see what assets the company has, how much it owes, how much is coming in as income and going out as expenses, and even how well it is managing the use of its cash. It's not good if the business is generating plenty of income but has no cash on hand to pay the bills. The complete financial statement also allows you to answer important questions about the business, such as whether it's producing enough income to cover expenses or whether it is relying on borrowing, whether it has cash on hand to pay the bills, whether it is collecting on the accounts receivable quickly enough and turning the income into usable cash, and so on.

Each statement provides different information.

**BALANCE SHEET**: Shows what assets are owned by the business, the amount of owner's equity in the business (for example, how much the partners paid to start/ buy into a practice or the amount of stock outstanding), and the amount of debt that the business owes.

**INCOME STATEMENT** (also called the profit and loss statement): Shows how much income the company is producing from its different income streams, as well as the amount of expenses created in producing that income and the net profit or loss.

**STATEMENT OF CASH FLOW**: Shows if cash is coming in from operating activities, investing activities, or from financing activities like borrowing; how much cash is on hand to pay bills; how much cash has been used during the reporting time period; and what exactly the cash is being used for.

---

**Remember:** A financial statement is not complete unless it has the following things from *at least the current period and the previous time period*:

1. **Balance sheet**
2. **Income statement** (profit & loss statement)
3. **Statement of cash flow**

Comparing several years will allow you to see if the business or investment is going in the right direction or whether something is askew that needs to be addressed before it becomes a large issue. For example, is the income growing and keeping up with the expenses or are the expenses eating away all of the income? Does the business need new revenue streams or does it need to cut costs? Where is the business getting its cash from—revenue or from bank borrowing? Is the company accumulating too much debt to where you should be concerned? Comparing all three statements together allows you to see a complete picture and see how well income is generated, how efficiently the money is being utilized, and how the cash is moved around the company. If one of the three statements is missing or you do not have at least two complete financial statements, you do not have a complete picture, and things can be easily missed or overlooked.

When learning to read financial statements, I recommend that you have a colored pen or pencil to draw lines under each section. It helps to break up each section and make the numbers seem less overwhelming. You can start by looking at the bottom-line numbers of each section first. If the bottom-line numbers look out of order, you can look at the individual numbers. Make sure to look at the entries that make up the bottom line to see if anything looks out of place. Also, you may have certain numbers that you want to be sure to look at every month, like A/R (accounts receivable) or the company credit line. Consider using a different color for each of the statements (balance sheet, income statement, and cash flow). By doing so, you can more easily compare your statements between time periods. This should allow you to quickly locate the needed numbers until you get the hang of where to find them in each of the statements. I'll provide examples further on as we discuss the three financial sections.

## BENCHMARKING

Benchmarking is where you compare one company against others in the same industry. So if you own a pediatric practice, you would compare your practice's numbers to the average pediatric practice numbers. For doctors, you can get these numbers from MGMA (Medical Group Management Association). If you see that your practice is deviating from the norm, you need to figure out why. The benchmark provides a standard against which your practice can be measured to determine if there are items that need to be addressed.

## FINANCIAL LITERACY: Double Entry Bookkeeping

It is impossible to discuss financial literacy without briefly discussing **double entry bookkeeping**. This just means that every transaction made in the accounting books will be entered under two separate accounts to keep the books "in balance." One entry goes in the "Debit" column and one in the "Credit" column.

For example, if a medical practice purchases an exam table for the office with cash, there will be an entry to decrease the cash account amount to purchase the table. There will also be an entry to increase the asset account of "office equipment" to show that the company now owns another asset, the table. So the practice still has the same overall amount of assets; it's just that the cash is lower and the office equipment is higher. That is double-entry bookkeeping. Not that hard, right? If the books balance, it does not necessarily mean that there have not been mistakes made or there is no fraud going on. So be on the lookout for entries that don't look right.

Now discussing credits and debits can be a bit more confusing. Depending on the account, the entry could be called a debit or a credit. Whether it is referred to as a debit or credit depends on which account it affects and if it raises or lowers the balance. It's important to at least understand the terminology and concepts and worry about learning which accounts the debits and credits raise and lower later, as you get used to reading financial statements. You will find that a credit does not always raise an account balance and a debit does not always lower an account balance. It depends on the account involved.

## FINANCIAL LITERACY: Current vs. Long-Term

**CURRENT** is anything within the next 12-month period and **LONG-TERM** is anything over 12 months. So current debt is debt due within the next 12 months; long-term debt is due in more than 12 months. For example, A/P (accounts payable), where you buy supplies on credit and pay the invoice later, will generally be due in 90 days or less and is classified as a current liability. Credit cards are also current liabilities. Long-term liability would include your mortgage payments if your practice owns a building, since it may take 20 years to pay off the building. But the rent or mortgage payments that will be due in the next 12 months will be listed under current debt.

### TAKEAWAYS

- A complete financial statement is made up of a balance sheet, income statement, and cash flow statement from the previous two or more time periods.
- Balance sheet shows who owns what and how much debt there is.
- Income sheet shows the profit and expenses that went into making it.
- Cash flow shows what the cash is being used for and where it is coming from.
- Compare your practice to the benchmark to see how well it is doing.

### TO-DO LIST

- ☐ Get a complete set of financial statements from the last two or three time periods.

- ☐ Familiarize yourself with the types of entries that your business has on the three financial sheets. Get your colored pens handy.

- ☐ Find a benchmark standard for your business and compare it yearly.

## FINANCIAL LITERACY: Cash-Basis vs. Accrual Accounting

There are two types of accounting that can be used: cash-basis and accrual.

**CASH-BASIS** means that a "sale" is only recorded when cash is received, and expenses are counted when the cash is actually paid out. For example, if you see a patient, and the insurance company doesn't pay for 60 days, the "sale" of seeing the patient is only recorded 60 days later, when you receive the insurance payment.

In **ACCRUAL ACCOUNTING**, the transaction or service is recorded at the time of service whether or not cash was received. For example, a patient visit is recorded on the day you see the patient and not when the insurance company decides to pay. This type of accounting helps match expenses and revenue. So when you see the patient in the office, the visit is recorded even though you still have not received cash payment, and any expenses related to that visit like injection materials are also recorded at the same time. Most large businesses and medical practices use accrual accounting.

The only thing that you need to remember is that you cannot mix the two when you are accounting for transactions.

# CHAPTER 12

# THE BALANCE SHEET

## (WHO OWNS WHAT?)

The first piece of the complete financial statement is the Balance Sheet. The balance sheet shows what the practice owns and what it owes. This chapter will look at the following topics:

- What Do You Find on the Balance Sheet?
- Delving Deeper into the Balance Sheet

## WHAT DO YOU FIND ON THE BALANCE SHEET?

Whether you're looking at your own practice's financial status or considering buying stock in a company, you need to know what assets the business owns and how much it owes to the bank. The balance sheet is where you find this information along with how much money the owners have put into the company.

The amount that the owners have put into the business is known as **owners' equity**. It may also show up as "stock" or even as "retained earnings" (money accumulated by the practice that is to be paid to the owners in the future or be re-invested into the business). Essentially, owners' equity is any money that is due to the owners that has not yet been paid out. It's an IOU. The balance sheet is also where you find how much and what the company owns by looking under **assets**. If the company has borrowed money to buy items for the practice, you will see how much is owed and to whom under **liabilities**.

The balance sheet equation is:

**OWNERS' EQUITY + LIABILITIES = ASSETS**

This statement must always stay "in balance." This means that the numbers on both sides of the equation should always equal the other side.

According to the equation above, if the practice buys an asset, the money to pay for that asset can only come from one of three places.

1. The owners' equity through the owners putting more money into the business
2. The bank or other lending institution (as a liability)
3. One asset being sold to buy another

If the business bought an asset like an exam table with cash, the overall equation will not change since the cash used is replaced with a different asset (the table that was purchased). If an asset is obtained without using cash, it must have been paid for by the bank (via a loan) or by the business owners (the owners put more money into the practice and owners' equity increases). Ideally, the business uses assets, like cash, to buy other assets. If you notice that the liabilities are rising higher each reporting period, you need to stop and ask, "Why? Is the business having issues generating revenue, or is it having a problem converting the accounts receivable to cash? Why does it need to borrow from the bank or tap the line of credit?" The "why things are happening" is more important than the actual numbers.

Let's look at an example balance sheet. The first image is one that has not been marked up and can be a bit tough to read. The second is the same statement, which has been marked up to draw attention to whatever numbers the professional cares about. In this case it is the A/R number, the inventory, and the liabilities. If you get used to marking up the statements, then you can easily locate the numbers that are important to you each month and compare them to previous statements. It's okay to mark up and draw all over the financial statements. They are your statements and it's your business.

# BALANCE SHEET
*(As of June 30, 2016)*

| ASSETS | JUNE 2016 | MAY 2016 | APRIL 2016 |
|---|---|---|---|
| **CURRENT ASSETS** | | | |
| Cash | 68,000 | 175,000 | 148,000 |
| Inventory | 11,000 | 9,000 | 13,000 |
| Accounts Receivable | 208,000 | 199,000 | 183,000 |
| **TOTAL CURRENT ASSETS** | **287,000** | **383,700** | **344,000** |
| | | | |
| **FIXED ASSETS** | | | |
| Office Equipment | 42,000 | 43,200 | 44,400 |
| Computer Equip. | 218,000 | 220,000 | 222,000 |
| Building and Land | 697,000 | 707,000 | 717,000 |
| **TOTAL FIXED ASSETS** | **957,000** | **970,200** | **983,400** |
| **TOTAL ASSETS** | **1,244,000** | **1,353,900** | **1,327,400** |
| | | | |
| **LIABILITIES** | | | |
| **CURRENT LIABILITIES** | | | |
| Accounts Payable | 5,800 | 7,300 | 7,600 |
| Line of Credit | 98,000 | 106,000 | 110,000 |
| Current Long-term Debt | 26,000 | 26,000 | 26,000 |
| **TOTAL CURRENT LIABILITIES** | **129,800** | **139,300** | **143,600** |
| | | | |
| **LONG-TERM LIABILITIES** | | | |
| Bank Loan – Equipment | 68,000 | 78,000 | 88,000 |
| Bank Loan - Building & Land | 321,000 | 337,000 | 353,000 |
| **TOTAL LONG-TERM LIABILITIES** | **389,000** | **415,000** | **441,000** |
| **TOTAL LIABILITIES** | **518,800** | **554,300** | **584,600** |
| | | | |
| **OWNERS' EQUITY** | | | |
| Common Stock | 160,000 | 160,000 | 160,000 |
| Retained Earnings | 565,200 | 639,600 | 582,800 |
| **TOTAL EQUITY** | **725,200** | **799,600** | **742,800** |
| **TOTAL LIABILITIES and OWNERS' EQUITY** | **1,244,000** | **1,353,900** | **1,327,400** |

YIKES! All of those numbers can seem overwhelming—here is where the colored pens come in handy. Under each of the sections or anything you want to track, draw a line under it all the way across and even box it. It helps to break the statement down visually (See page 133).

In the left-hand column, under ASSETS, you will find what the medical practice owns. For example, under assets you may find accounts receivable, cash, land or buildings the practice owns, drugs and supplies, computers and EMRs (electronic medical records), as well as items like tables and stools, and even intangible items like patents. One of the most important items for a medical practice is accounts receivable (A/R) which is found on the balance sheet. This is because the majority of payments will initially be recorded as A/R. We will take a more in-depth look at the A/R later on.

If you look at the liabilities and owners' equity area of the balance sheet and compare it with the previous statement, you can see whether the practice has used financing or cash, or whether the owners had to invest more money to buy those assets. You can see how leveraged the practice is; that is, how much of the assets are financed with debt. You want a business that has adequate cash, with assets that are financed with cash and equity instead of with liabilities. Highly leveraged companies (with high debt amounts) are much more risky that those with a high level of cash on the balance sheet. This goes for publicly traded companies and investments as well as your own practice.

## DELVING DEEPER INTO THE BALANCE SHEET

Once you have evaluated the overall balance sheet, you need to delve deeper to get a better picture of the practice's financial health. There are several ratios that can help you. Banks and lending institutions look at these numbers to see how liquid the practice is (the ability to cover its debt with cash or cash equivalents) and to see how well the business is managing assets prior to granting a loan. They will determine if the business is using its assets like cash to purchase other assets or if it has to rely on debt.

**QUICK RATIO** (also known as the acid ratio) helps you determine how liquid a company is. It will tell you if the practice has the **quick assets** to cover the current liabilities. Quick assets are those that can be "quickly"

# BALANCE SHEET
*(As of June 30, 2016)*

| ASSETS | JUNE 2016 | MAY 2016 | APRIL 2016 |
|---|---|---|---|
| **CURRENT ASSETS** | | | |
| Cash | 68,000 | 175,000 | 148,000 |
| Inventory | 11,000 | 9,000 | 13,000 |
| Accounts Receivable | 208,000 | 199,000 | 183,000 |
| **TOTAL CURRENT ASSETS** | **287,000** | **383,700** | **344,000** |
| | | | |
| **FIXED ASSETS** | | | |
| Office Equipment | 42,000 | 43,200 | 44,400 |
| Computer Equip. | 218,000 | 220,000 | 222,000 |
| Building and Land | 697,000 | 707,000 | 717,000 |
| **TOTAL FIXED ASSETS** | **957,000** | **970,200** | **983,400** |
| **TOTAL ASSETS** | **1,244,000** | **1,353,900** | **1,327,400** |
| | | | |
| **LIABILITIES** | | | |
| **CURRENT LIABILITIES** | | | |
| Accounts Payable | 5,800 | 7,300 | 7,600 |
| Line of Credit | 98,000 | 106,000 | 110,000 |
| Current Long- term Debt | 26,000 | 26,000 | 26,000 |
| **TOTAL CURRENT LIABILITIES** | **129,800** | **139,300** | **143,600** |
| | | | |
| **LONG-TERM LIABILITIES** | | | |
| Bank Loan – Equipment | 68,000 | 78,000 | 88,000 |
| Bank Loan - Building & Land | 321,000 | 337,000 | 353,000 |
| **TOTAL LONG-TERM LIABILITIES** | **389,000** | **415,000** | **441,000** |
| **TOTAL LIABILITIES** | **518,800** | **554,300** | **584,600** |
| | | | |
| **OWNERS' EQUITY** | | | |
| Common Stock | 160,000 | 160,000 | 160,000 |
| Retained Earnings | 565,200 | 639,600 | 582,800 |
| **TOTAL EQUITY** | **725,200** | **799,600** | **742,800** |
| **TOTAL LIABILITIES and OWNERS' EQUITY** | **1,244,000** | **1,353,900** | **1,327,400** |

turned into cash, and current liabilities are those that are "quickly" coming due in the next 12 months. These assets in a medical practice usually include cash and A/R (accounts receivable). Banks and investors like to see a large amount of cash to debt because they will be more likely to get their money back if something should happen to the company.

How liquid is my practice?

**QUICK RATIO = QUICK ASSETS (cash and A/R) ÷ CURRENT LIABILITIES**

The Quick Ratio should be greater than one. If the number is less than one, the practice will not have enough cash to pay its current bills. Be aware that a practice can manipulate numbers, like using the "charged" A/R numbers (which in a medical practice may be inflated 200%–400%) instead of using what the practice realistically expects to collect. This overinflates the numbers and makes the financial picture appear rosier than it really is.

**DEBT-TO-ASSET RATIO** shows the degree to which the practice is **leveraged**, that is, using debt to pay for items instead of using cash. Debt-to-Asset ratio is very similar to the quick ratio but uses all assets and liabilities.

How leveraged is my practice?

**DEBT-TO-ASSET RATIO = TOTAL DEBT ÷ TOTAL ASSETS**

For example, the practice has $40,000 in debt and $100,000 in assets. The debt-to-asset ratio would be 0.4, or in other words, 40% of the practice's assets are financed by debt and not owned outright by the company. Less than .035-.5 is ideal. Once the number gets in the range of .5-1, banks and other lenders begin to worry about the practice being able to cover its debts and repay the loan. All ratio numbers of the practice should be compared against benchmark standards. Your practice manager should be able to produce these numbers for you. Make sure that you understand where the numbers came from that went into figuring out the ratios. Because garbage in equals garbage out, you want to make sure the numbers used are appropriate and accurate.

If you find that your practice has high amounts of debt and therefore a very high debt-to-asset ratio, you may be looking at trouble. If the ratio is large or getting larger compared with previous time periods, or is much higher than a benchmark standard, you need to figure out why the business has to obtain loans to pay for items. Is the revenue too low? Are expenses too high? Is it having issues converting accounts receivable to cash? Or perhaps the practice recently bought a large item like an MRI machine that will generate income. In that case, perhaps the high debt-to-asset ratio is okay in the short term. Again, the higher the ratio, the more leveraged the company and the more risk there is.

## FINANCIAL LITERACY: Depreciation/Amortization Terms

These two terms pertain to how a practice accounts for the utilization of equipment, factories, computers, or other physical assets, or something intangible like a patent or goodwill to the point that it becomes worthless. When you purchase a computer system, it goes onto the accounting books, but at some point the computer will become obsolete. So once it is obsolete and you need to buy a new one, how do you get the old one off of the books? In comes depreciation and amortization.

Depreciation does two things. The first is that it gets rid of items from the accounting books that get used up or become obsolete. It does this by expensing them slowly over several years. In the accounting system, you will have a certain decrease in the item's value each year until it is worth nothing. (There are rules as to how fast you can decrease the value of the item and over what length of time period that we will not get into here.) For example, a computer asset may be worth $1,000 initially and its useful life is considered to be five years. And equal depreciation will be taken each year. So

*(continued on next page)*

(continued from previous page)

each year it is worth $200 less on the books until year six when it is worth nothing and has been used up. (And since this is accounting, there has to be two entries for the double bookkeeping. So the flip side of the decrease in the computer value is a column called depreciation.) The "computer depreciation" line item will increase by the same amount as the decrease of the computer value in the asset column. So at the end of year two, the computer is "worth" $600 and the computer depreciation expense column will be $400.

Here's where it gets a little tricky. Depreciation is treated as an expense because it is being used to offset the value of the computer on the books. Because it is treated as an expense, it will lower your overall revenue for the year. Why would you want that? It is a good thing for a business, because it will lower the income that it will have to pay tax on that year.

Because it lowers income, the books can get cooked to make them look better by changing how fast items are depreciated. So if you want to make income look better, you slow down depreciating an item so the numbers aren't beaten down by the depreciation expense and the income will appear higher.

The same is true if you are looking at having a very large income for the year and want to shelter it from tax. You could change the depreciation schedule to decrease the income by taking a larger than normal depreciation expense. Both of these scenarios are frowned upon.

For example, a business has $200,000 in income for each of the last two years. It has a $100,000 piece of equipment it is depreciating over five years. The manager decides to take an even depreciation rate over the five years. So this year he will take $20,000 as a depreciation expense, which makes the income appear as $180,000 on it's taxes.

If instead he takes an accelerated depreciation of $30,000, that year the income will appear as $170,000. So to the untrained eye, it will appear that the revenue decreased from the previous year. If you

(continued on next page)

[continued from previous page]

understand the depreciation, you realize that the drop in income is not real and only due to the depreciation expense.

Now let's say that the business revenue has fallen this year to $190,000 and you have an unscrupulous manager who decides to prop up the income so he doesn't alarm the owners. He does not take the appropriate depreciation and instead only takes $10,000 this year. This makes the income look like it is still the same as the previous year at $180,000 despite the income actually going down. You need to be aware of these schemes.

By the way, the IRS frowns upon manipulating depreciation to avoid taxes. You do need to be aware of potential manipulation so you can look at the depreciation column and see if it seems the same from year to year. If you notice the manager changing the depreciation schedule, then you need to know why he is doing it. Is there a problem that they are covering up? Or is it a legitimate reason, done in a legal way?

Amortization is the same as depreciation, but it applies to non-tangible items like goodwill (value of your brand), patents, trademarks, and so on. Basically anything that you cannot touch but has value that will eventually expire will undergo amortization and is treated in the same manner as a depreciation expense.

## TAKEAWAYS

- The balance sheet shows what the business owns (assets), what it owes (liabilities), and how much money the owners have invested (owners' equity).
- Use debt-to-asset ratio to determine how leveraged your practice is, and the quick ratio to see how liquid it is.
- Depreciation and amortization are used to account for assets becoming obsolete.

**TO-DO LIST**

☐   Familiarize yourself with what your business owns and owes.

☐   Decide what numbers are important to you; get your handy pens out and start marking up the financial statements.

# CHAPTER 13

# THE INCOME STATEMENT

## *(HOW MUCH DID I MAKE?)*

The second piece of the financial statement is the income statement. As the name implies, the income statement looks at whether or not the practice is producing an income. The bottom-line number on this statement is usually the first and only thing many professionals look at to see how their practice is doing. They look to see if there is a profit or a loss. Uninformed professionals believe incorrectly that their practice is doing well if the bottom-line number is positive. You need to understand why the number is positive or negative. In this chapter we will look at the following:

- Why Don't We Look at Only the Bottom Line?
- What Do You Find on the Income Statement?
- The Steps of the Income Statement
- Delving Deeper into the Income Statement: Testing Profitability

## WHY DON'T WE LOOK AT ONLY THE BOTTOM LINE?

The income statement's bottom line number tells you if there was a profit or a loss for the time period. The income statement is therefore also known as a profit and loss statement (P&L). If the bottom-line number is positive, you need to understand *why* the business is making a profit, and if it is negative you need to know *why* it is running at a loss. Even if the practice has a profit, you should examine the items that create the bottom-line number and compare those with the previous time period. Understand that profit = income = *net* earnings. These terms are generally used inter-changeably and refer to the same thing. Be aware that net income is not the same as income or net earnings. This is jargon you have to get used to.

A practice could be in financial difficulty while still posting a profit. The bottom line might be positive, but the expenses and overhead could be outpacing the revenue. If you compare it to the last two-to-three years or time periods, you may notice that the overhead has ballooned while the revenue has meagerly increased, and if not corrected, the practice may soon be operating at a loss. Alternatively, a practice could show a loss, but the business is doing well. Depreciation expense or a large one-time purchase may make the bottom line appear low and the business appear to be doing poorly even though it is thriving. You always need to compare it to previous time periods to determine what is causing the bottom-line change and determine if corrective action needs to be taken.

**FINANCIAL LITERACY: What is COGS?**

**COGS = COST OF GOODS SOLD**

**COGS** reflects only the expenses that go into actually producing the income. So for physicians, COGS is the cost of seeing patients, providing DME (durable medical equipment), doing injections, giving vaccines, performing x-rays, and so on. This includes the costs for patient gowns, gloves to examine patients, syringes for injections, DME, med-tech salaries, and so on; anything that is *directly* related to seeing patients or producing revenue. This does not include practice manager's salary, building rent, or utilities, which fall under **operating expenses**.

**FINANCIAL LITERACY: The difference between GROSS and NET**

**GROSS is the larger of the two.** For example, **GROSS INCOME** is the amount *before* you have removed the expenses, and so on.

**NET is the smaller of the two amounts and is what is left over.** For example, **NET INCOME** is the amount left *after* you have deducted the costs and expenses, and so on. The net is always a *smaller* number than the gross.

## WHAT DO YOU FIND ON THE INCOME STATEMENT?

On an income statement, you will find the items that go into making a profit or creating a loss. These include any revenue brought in, expenses that go into making that revenue called COGS (Cost of Goods Sold), expenses called operating expenses that occur whether or not revenue is produced, depreciation, and taxes.

An income statement generally looks like what is shown on the following pages. (Don't be alarmed at how many lines of numbers there are.) Keep in mind that all you are really dealing with is income and expenses. The expenses are broken down into those that are related to producing an income, like seeing patients or clients, and those expenses that occur whether or not you do any business, like renting office space.

There are two formats you may see. These are the single-step format and the multi-step format.

## SINGLE-STEP FORMAT

REVENUE
　　*−EXPENSES*

INCOME

## MULTI-STEP FORMAT

NET REVENUE
　*- COGS*

GROSS PROFIT (related to seeing patients or clients)
　*- OPERATING EXPENSES    (rent, etc.)*

OPERATING INCOME
　　OTHER INCOME
　　　*- OTHER EXPENSES*

INCOME BEFORE TAXES
　　　*- INCOME TAX*

NET INCOME    (what's left over)

Next are examples of the two formats.

# MULTI-STEP FORMAT

## INCOME STATEMENT
*(as of June 30, 2016)*

| NET REVENUE | JUNE 2016 | MAY 2016 | APRIL 2016 |
|---|---|---|---|
| MD Charges | 264,400 | 273,800 | 261,000 |
| Mid-level Provider Charges | 44,400 | 41,000 | 49,500 |
| Sales – medical equipment | 9,300 | 12,200 | 9,500 |
| Mid level Salaries | (13,200) | (13,200) | (13,200) |
| Med Tech Salaries | (28,000) | (28,000) | (28,000) |
| Radiology Salaries | (6,500) | (6,500) | (6,500) |
| Medical Supply Costs | (5,200) | (6,400) | (4,200) |
| Drugs / Medications | (1,400) | (1,100) | (1,300) |
| **GROSS PROFIT** | **263,800** | **271,800** | **266,800** |
| | | | |
| **OPERATING EXPENSES** | | | |
| Office Salaries | (58,000) | (58,000) | (58,000) |
| Advertisement | (2,100) | (0) | (2,100) |
| Office Supplies | (1,700) | (1,100) | (1,800) |
| Utilities | (900) | (900) | (1,000) |
| Equipment Expense | (10,000) | (10,000) | (10,000) |
| Building Expense | (16,000) | (16,000) | (16,000) |
| **OPERATING INCOME** | **175,100** | **185,800** | **177,900** |
| | | | |
| **Other Income** | **200** | **0** | **1,000** |
| | | | |
| **Other Expense** | 0 | 0 | 0 |
| Interest | (7,700) | (7,700) | (7,700) |
| Depreciation | (13,200 | (13,200) | (13,200) |
| **INCOME BEFORE TAXES** | **154,400** | **164,900** | **158,100** |
| | | | |
| **Income Taxes** | (17,800) | (17,800) | (17,800) |
| **NET INCOME/NET PROFIT** | 136,600 | 147,100 | 140,200 |

## SINGLE-STEP FORMAT

### INCOME STATEMENT
*(as of June 30, 2016)*

| REVENUE | JUNE 2016 | MAY 2016 | APRIL 2016 |
|---|---|---|---|
| MD Charges | 264,400 | 273,800 | 261,000 |
| Mid-level Provider Charges | 44,400 | 41,000 | 49,500 |
| Sales – medical equipment | 9,300 | 12,200 | 9,500 |
| Other Income | 200 | 0 | 1,000 |
| TOTAL REVENUE | 318,300 | 327,000 | 321,000 |
| | | | |
| EXPENSES | | | |
| Mid level Salaries | 13,200 | 13,200 | 13,200 |
| Med-Tech Salaries | 28,000 | 28,000 | 28,000 |
| Radiology Salaries | 6,500 | 6,500 | 6,500 |
| Medical Supply Costs | 5,200 | 6,400 | 4,200 |
| Drugs/ Medications | 1,400 | 1,100 | 1,300 |
| Office Salaries | 58,000 | 58,000 | 58,000 |
| Advertisement | 2,100 | 0 | 2,100 |
| Office Supplies | 1,700 | 1,100 | 1,800 |
| Utilities | 900 | 900 | 1,000 |
| Equipment Expense | 10,000 | 10,000 | 10,000 |
| Building Expense | 16,000 | 16,000 | 16,000 |
| Interest | 7,700 | 7,700 | 7,700 |
| Depreciation | 13,200 | 13,200 | 13,200 |
| Income Taxes | 17,800 | 17,800 | 17,800 |
| TOTAL EXPENSES | 181,700 | 179,900 | 180,800 |
| NET INCOME/NET PROFIT | 136,600 | 147,100 | 140,200 |

Again, don't forget to use the colored pens to mark the numbers you are most interested in.

The single-step format has less jargon and is easier to follow when looking through the numbers. But the multi-step format makes it easier to crunch more advanced numbers and ratios so you can determine how well and efficiently the practice is running. Regardless of which you or your accountant chooses, keep it the same each time and pull out the colored pens until you get used to looking at these statements.

## THE STEPS OF THE INCOME STATEMENT

Let's discuss each step of the statement. The top line is the Net Revenue or Net Sales number from seeing patients or clients, but it is usually listed as just "revenue." The reason it is net instead of gross is because this number takes into account any discounts or refunds that may have occurred already that decreased the overall gross revenue number.

The first step is subtraction of the expenses that are directly tied to seeing those patients or clients. Again, this is known as **COGS** (cost of goods sold) and includes any expense that is directly related to producing the revenue. The result of subtracting the cost of seeing patients and clients from the net revenue is the **gross profit**.

What is left over is what the practice uses to pay the **operating expenses**. Operating expenses include anything not making revenue, such as the rent, managers' salaries, utilities, postage, and so on. These have to be paid whether or not you are producing revenue. The result of subtracting the operating expenses from the gross profit is **operating income**. This is what is left over after paying for the expenses related to seeing patients and clients and expenses related to operating the business.

If you have any additional income from investments, you add it in after the operating expenses. After that, the next step is subtraction of interest payments on loans and the depreciation expenses, which will give you **income before taxes**. The last step is to subtract the taxes, which leaves you with the **net income or net profit**.

By examining the income statement and comparing it with several years, you can determine the following.

- Is the practice making a profit or loss?
- What direction and magnitude is the change of that profit or loss?

- What revenue streams are there? And do they appear to be productive?
- What are all of the expenses that the practice pays? Do the costs seem to be controlled and appropriate?
- Is depreciation being deducted appropriately?
- Are the appropriate taxes being paid?
- How profitable is the company?
- What is the overhead percentage?

If you see that the revenues are off, you need to delve deeper and find out why. Are you seeing fewer patients or clients, are the insurance reimbursements decreasing, or perhaps the practice is not collecting co-pays and co-insurance from patients or clients are being seen without paying? Maybe the practice needs to evaluate additional revenue streams to improve the profit margins. Are some of the revenue streams not productive? The income statement also allows you to evaluate your costs. Are your costs of supplies or rent and utilities increasing? Do you need to determine if the number of patients/clients being seen at the practice has fallen and perhaps now it has too many staff members? Or perhaps the depreciation schedule was increased or a large one-time purchase made. Make sure you skim the items listed under the expenses to make sure they seem appropriate. That way you can get a good handle on what your practice is spending money on and see if there are any ways to cut expenses or boost revenues. It's very similar to your going over your personal credit card and bank statements each month to see what you have been buying and if there are any funny-looking charges on your statement.

## DELVING DEEPER INTO THE INCOME STATEMENT: TESTING PROFITABILITY

After you have determined that the business is making a profit and why that is so, you need to see how profitable it is. The profitability numbers can then be compared to benchmark standards to see how well the business stacks up.

## NET PROFIT MARGIN

The net profit margin is a number that reflects the percentage of the revenue or sales that the business gets to keep after all of the expenses are paid. It allows you to compare the profitability of different practices.

How profitable is my practice?
**NET PROFIT MARGIN = NET PROFIT ÷ NET REVENUE**

For example, your practice has net profit (bottom line number) of $400,000 and net revenue (top line number) of $1,000,000. The net profit margin is 40%. Compare this with benchmarks for your specialty.

## OVERHEAD RATE

This is a very common number for professionals to keep track of against the benchmarks. In general, medical practices will lump COGS and the operating expenses together for Total Operating Expenses to calculate the overhead rate. Most practices tend to treat physician assistants and nurse practitioners as staff for this calculation. The Total Operating Expenses do not include professionals' salaries or their fringe benefits unless they are employees. Essentially it includes all expenses except owners' salaries and benefits, interest, depreciation, and taxes. Here is how you calculate your overhead rate.

**OVERHEAD RATE =**
**TOTAL OPERATING EXP (COGS + OPERATING EXP)**
**÷ NET REVENUE**

If your overhead rate is larger than the benchmark for your practice type (pediatrics, podiatry, chiropractic, elder law, dentistry, etc.), it may mean one of three things. The first is that your expenses are too high and need to be reduced. The second is that your revenue may be low and needs to be boosted. The worst-case scenario is that your expenses are too high and your revenue is too low. As always, you need to understand why the number is the amount that it is and in which direction it is trending so it can be corrected, if needed.

## TAKEAWAYS

- The income statement shows what the revenues are, the expenses incurred to produce the revenues, recurring operating expenses, and whether there is a profit or a loss.
- Do not concern yourself with the bottom-line number but be concerned with *why* that number is positive or negative.
- Net profit margin is used to determine profitability.
- You can compare the overhead rate to the benchmark to see if your expenses are in line with the average.

## TO-DO LIST

- ❏ Familiarize yourself with where your revenue comes from and what expenses are incurred to make that revenue.
- ❏ Decide what numbers are important to you; get your handy pens out and start marking up the financial statements.

# CHAPTER 14

# THE STATEMENT OF CASH FLOW

## *(WHERE DID ALL OF THE CASH GO?)*

The third and final piece of the financial statement is the statement of cash flow, which focuses on the movement of cash throughout the business. This chapter looks at the following topics:

- What Do You Find on the Statement of Cash Flow?
- Indirect or Direct Method of Reporting
- Delving Deeper into the Cash Flow Statement

## WHAT DO YOU FIND ON THE STATEMENT OF CASH FLOW?

The statement of cash flow tracks the movement of your cash. It tells you how liquid the practice is (cash on hand) and in turn how well it can cover the bills. This statement shows how the practice generates cash—from the practice's business activities, from investing activities, or from borrowing activities. It shows how the company spent cash and reveals how much cash is on hand at the end of the period. Making cash is the main business of a practice, and without it a practice cannot pay its bills. On the income statement, it is possible for the practice to appear to be doing well, with a profitable bottom line. But when you examine the statement of cash flow, you realize that the practice has little to no cash flow from its business operations and is relying on borrowing to subsidize the cash flow. The statement of cash flow gives a snapshot in time and must be compared with the cash flow statements from several previous time periods.

Cash in a company can be generated from or used for three business activities:

1. **Operating** or business activities, which include turnover of A/R (accounts receivable), paying down A/P (accounts payable), buying or selling inventories, and collecting cash receipts from patients and clients
2. **Investing** activities that involve buying and selling equipment/buildings, and so on, or securities like stocks
3. **Financing** activities that involve raising money from new partners, buying out old partners, or taking on more loans or paying them off

## INDIRECT OR DIRECT REPORTING METHOD

The statement of cash flow is reported either by the **indirect method** or the **direct method**. The "indirect" and "direct" methods apply *only* to the operational activities section. The investing and financing sections are the same in both. Remember, the direct method reports actual account values, whereas the indirect method reports only changes in the account values. Because the direct method shows the actual amounts of cash and expenses, it gives away a lot of information. Most publicly traded companies will only use the indirect method to report so they don't give away as much information to their competitors. In the indirect method you will find depreciation expense added back in because it is an expense that was not actually paid out. Examples of the two methods are shown below.

# INDIRECT METHOD

The indirect method shows only the change in cash value instead of the actual cash amount. The operating section for the indirect method looks like the following. Remember the Financing and Investing sections are the same in both.

**CASH FLOW – OPERATING ACTIVITIES**
NET INCOME (or loss)
    Changes in Accounts Receivable (A/R)
    Changes in Depreciation
    Changes in Inventories (Drugs, DME, etc.)
    Changes in Accounts Payable (A/P)
    Changes in current liabilities (rent, loan, etc. due next 12mths)

**NET CASH provided by or used in Operating activities**

**CASH FLOW – INVESTING ACTIVITIES**
    Changes in Assets (purchase/sale of equipment, buildings, etc.)
    Sale or purchase of securities or other investments

**NET CASH provided by or used in investing activities**

**CASH FLOW – FINANCING ACTIVITIES**
    Changes in Practice Stock (partner buy-in/out)
    Changes in Retained Earnings (payout or increase)
    Changes in Debt (long-term loans, credit lines)

**NET CASH provided by or used in financing activities**
**NET CHANGE IN CASH PROVIDED BY ALL ACTIVITIES**

# DIRECT METHOD

The direct method is more transparent than the indirect method. However, it takes more effort to create the direct method.

---

**CASH FLOW – OPERATING ACTIVITIES**

    Cash from patients

    Cash from insurance companies

    Cash paid to vendors for supplies

    Cash paid for debt service payments

    Cash paid for employees and staff salaries

    Income tax paid

---

**CASH ON HAND FROM OPERATING ACTIVITIES**

Since many practices will use an indirect method, we will only look at an example of an indirect method cash flow statement.

Operational activities include anything associated with your actual business. These include changes in accounts receivable, accounts payable, cash deposits, inventories, other current liabilities, and the addition of depreciation back in (indirect method only).

Investing activities involve using cash to purchase items like MRIs, X-ray equipment, buildings, and so on, or to purchase securities like stocks and bonds. They also include cash generated from the sale of a building, equipment, or securities.

# EXAMPLE OF THE INDIRECT METHOD

## CASH FLOW STATEMENT
*(As of June 30, 2016)*

| CASH FLOW – OPERATING ACTIVITIES | JUNE 2016 | MAY 2016 | APRIL 2016 |
|---|---|---|---|
| NET INCOME | 136,600 | 147,100 | 140,300 |
| Change in A/R | (9,000) | (16,000) | 21,000 |
| Change in A/P | (1,500) | (300) | (1,200) |
| Change in Inventories | (2,000) | 4,000 | (1,800) |
| Change in Current Liabilities | (9,500) | (4,300) | (11,200) |
| Accumulated Depreciation | 13,200 | 13,200 | 13,200 |
| **NET CASH PROVIDED/USED IN OPERATING ACTIVITIES** | **127,800** | **143,700** | **160,300** |

| CASH FLOW – INVESTING ACTIVITIES | | | |
|---|---|---|---|
| Purchases or Sales of Equipment or Property | 0 | 0 | 0 |
| Other Investing Activity Purchase or Sales | 0 | 0 | 0 |
| **NET CASH PROVIDED/USED in INVESTING ACTIVITIES** | **0** | **0** | **0** |

| CASH FLOW – FINANCING ACTIVITIES | | | |
|---|---|---|---|
| Net Cash Provided/Used in Debt Activities | (35,500) | (30,300) | (38,000) |
| Buy Back / Sale of Stock | 0 | 0 | 0 |
| Payout Retained Earnings | (200,000) | 0 | (150,000) |
| **NET CASH PROVIDED/USED in FINANCING ACTIVITIES** | **(235,500)** | **(30,300)** | **(188,00)** |
| **NET CASH PROVIDED/ USED IN ALL ACTIVITIES** | **(107,700)** | **113,400** | **(27,700)** |

Financing activities include changes in the credit line amount outstanding, changes in the amount of long-term debt, new stock issues (new partner buying into the practice), or stock buy-back (buying an old partner out of the practice). Look to see if the practice is taking on more debt to get by or if it is doing well and paying down the line of credit and long-term debt. At the end of the year, many practices will divide any remaining cash among the owners and deplete the cash to almost zero. Because of this, there is little to no cash reserves on January 1, and it is commonplace for a practice to use the line of credit to pay the bills until the cash payments flow back in. Just watch to make sure that the line of credit is being paid down in a reasonable time frame. If it is toward the end of the year and the line of credit hasn't been paid down yet, you need to know why. The practice may be having cash flow issues.

A brief word about the change in the amount of cash vs. the change in the amount of inventories, A/R, and A/P: The change in cash and the account values is not always intuitive for people. If your practice's accounts receivable increases, your cash decreases. Most people think that if A/R increases they have been more productive, and the cash should have gone up, too. Do not confuse cash with A/R. A/R has the possibility to become cash, but has not been converted yet. The same is true for supply inventories. If you purchase supplies with cash, the cash will go down. If you purchase items with credit, the A/P (accounts payable) increases and your cash may stay the same or increase. This happens because in the current period the practice bought items on credit and kept its cash. But presumably next period the bill will be paid and the cash will decrease.

## DELVING DEEPER INTO THE CASH FLOW STATEMENT

The cash flow statement is also used to determine if your practice has enough cash to cover its debt via the cash-to-debt ratios. Remember, your accountant or practice manager should be able to calculate these numbers for you. You need to make sure of where the numbers came from and be sure to look at the results.

## CASH-TO-DEBT RATIOS

The **current cash-to-debt ratio** is a number that tells you if you have enough cash on hand to cover your short-term debt obligations in the next 12 months. If you do not, there is a serious problem with cash flow.

**Does your practice have enough cash to cover short-term debt?**

Calculate...

(Current Liabilities + Last Year Current Liabilities) ÷ 2 = Average Current Liabilities

Then...

CASH FROM OPERATING ACTIVITIES ÷

AVERAGE CURRENT LIABILITIES =

CURRENT CASH-TO-DEBT RATIO

You can also determine the TOTAL CASH-TO-DEBT ratio by using the same equation above but using both current and long-term liabilities instead of just current liabilities to figure out the Average Liabilities.

**How well can your practice cover all of its debt?**

Calculate...

(Liabilities this year + Last Year's) ÷ 2 = Average Liabilities

Then...

CASH FROM OPERATING ACTIVITIES ÷

AVERAGE LIABILITIES =

TOTAL CASH-TO-DEBT RATIO

The Total Cash-To-Debt Ratio tells you what the practice's ability is to pay both short- and long-term debt. If the long-term debt levels are too high, the practice may be in peril down the road. Have your practice manager calculate these numbers for you and compare them with previous time periods to see if the cash flow is improving.

## TAKEAWAYS

- Just because you are making a profit does not mean your practice is in good financial standing. You must have adequate cash flow or your business will be in trouble.
- Cash will come from or be used for operational activities, investing activities, or financing activities.
- Cash-to-debt ratios tell if there is enough cash on hand to cover the debt the practice has, both in the short and the long term.

## TO-DO LIST

- ❏ Familiarize yourself with where your cash comes from and what it is for.
- ❏ Have the cash-to-debt ratios calculated and compare them to the benchmarks and previous time periods.

# CHAPTER 15

# SUMMING UP BASIC FINANCIAL STATEMENTS AND DELVING DEEPER INTO ACCOUNTS RECEIVABLE

n the preceding chapters, we took an in-depth look at the three essential components of a complete financial statement. Now we need to put them all together to get an overall picture of the financial health of the company. This chapter will look at the following topics:

- Financial Statement Review
- Delving Deeper into Accounts Receivable (A/R)

## FINANCIAL STATEMENT REVIEW

Let's review what constitutes a complete financial statement. You need a balance sheet, income statement, and a cash flow statement for the current time period and at least two-to-three previous time periods. If you don't have that at a minimum, you cannot make any conclusions about how your practice is doing. Remember that these same rules about reading your practice's financial statement also apply for any investments you might be evaluating, such as stock investments, real estate deals, or investments in other companies. All of these should have financial statements. If they are produced before the investment has any income, they will be called a proforma. If you are reading a proforma or a public company's financial statement, *always make sure to read the fine print*, because that is where all of the details will be kept.

Remember, the balance sheet shows the amount and type of assets owned by the practice, including cash and A/R. It also shows the amount of liabilities and debts the practice owes, how much of the owners' money has been invested into the practice, and any retained earnings not yet paid out to the owners. You want to know how leveraged the company is that you are evaluating and what type of assets there are in case your investment goes bad. If the company has minimal debt to assets, then the likelihood of your losing your investment is less than if it is highly leveraged.

The income statement shows the net sales/revenue and expenses, depreciation, and taxes. It shows if there is an overall net profit/loss by the practice. By comparing these numbers to the preceding year, you can see if the numbers are moving in the wrong direction and need correction before they affect the bottom line. Do not get suckered into looking only at the bottom line. Make sure to see that the product or service lines are producing increasing revenue and that the expenses the business is incurring are not outpacing that revenue.

The statement of cash flow shows how much cash the practice has on hand to pay bills, where it is coming from, and what it is being used for. If you don't have cash, you can't pay your bills, and you have no reason to be in business. The sole purpose of a business is to make cash. Pay special attention to this statement. Remember that this is only a snapshot of the cash at the time you take it. It can change daily. If you are looking at an investment, you want to make sure that the business is not only producing good revenue but that it has adequate cash flow to pay the dividends or profits back to you, the investor.

The BALANCE SHEET will show you the following when compared with previous time periods:

1. How much your practice is worth, or the *net value*.
2. The amount of A/R, cash, inventory/supplies, and other assets that you can compare to previous time periods to see if they are increasing or decreasing.
3. The amount of debt, both short-term and long-term, that the business owes.

4.  How much money is owed to the owners (owners' equity and retained earnings).
5.  The liquidity of the practice, by using the *quick ratio* to see if the quick assets like cash can cover the current liabilities.

The INCOME STATEMENT will show the following when compared with previous time periods:

1.  The gross profit and net income changes.
2.  The increase or decrease in sales/revenues.
3.  The types and amounts of expenses the practice incurs.
4.  Figuring out the net profit margin will allow you to benchmark against other practices and follow the practice's profitability.
5.  Calculating the overhead rate will allow you to track the practice's expenses.

The CASH FLOW STATEMENT will show you the following when compared with previous time periods:

1.  The amount of cash that came in and went out over a time period.
2.  Any change in the financing activities like repayment of a loan or acquisition of a new loan.
3.  Any change in cash from investing like stock sale or repurchase.
4.  If there is enough cash to cover current expenses.

## DELVING DEEPER INTO THE ACCOUNTS RECEIVABLE

The majority of payments for services provided in a medical practice will be in the form of accounts receivable (A/R). Other types of practices, like law and veterinarian practices may have less in the way of A/R and more in the way of cash receipts. For practices that have large A/R accounts, A/R turnover into cash is very important. The A/R account can be a make-or-break account for a practice depending on how well it can be converted into cash. The majority of medical payments coming from insurance companies go into the A/R account before they are paid. The charges sit in accounts receivable until the payments are issued to the practice. Considering that a large percentage of income can be tied up in A/R, a practice that is unable to convert the A/R into cash may have issues paying the bills. Keeping on top of how quickly the A/R is converted to cash is important in avoiding cash flow issues.

When looking at accounts receivable, you need to make sure that the amount being recorded is the actual *expected* A/R amount and not an over-inflated amount that may be billed to insurance companies. For example, in medical practices it is common for charges to be inflated 200%–400%, even though realistically they expect to collect much less. So if the charge goes out as $300 but only $100 is the actual expected payment from the insurance company, it is important that the A/R is recorded as $100. If it's not recorded that way, the practice could appear to be doing better than it is due to overinflated revenues and A/R.

The practice also needs to keep track of how long the A/R sits there before the claim is paid. If it is taking longer than 30 days to be paid, you need to know why. Are the claims going to the insurance company improperly filled out? Is it only a particular insurance company that is slow to pay? (Perhaps the practice needs to decide not to accept that insurance if the company never pays its claims on time.) Also, how fast are patients paying? Maybe the practice needs to have a policy of collecting patient or client payments up front before services are rendered. It is horrible to have to go after patients or clients after the fact, and the likelihood of getting paid dramatically decreases once they receive the services they need.

If you are having issues collecting on the A/R in a timely fashion, the practice may have issues paying the bills unless the process is sped up. The practice may need to institute new payment policies or change how it sends out claims to insurance companies. Or perhaps it needs to offer discounts for patients who pay cash up front. It is easier and cheaper to collect money up front than have to go after it later.

A particularly important ratio is the **A/R TURNOVER RATIO** and the **number of days to collect the A/R**. They are calculated as follows.

Before your eyes roll back in your head with the thoughts of having to calculate this, again management should be able to calculate all of these

**How many days for company to collect on the A/R?**

Calculate...

(last year A/R+ current year A/R) ÷ 2 = Average A/R

Then...

**ANNUAL A/R SALES ÷ AVERAGE A/R
= A/R TURNOVER RATIO**

Then...

**52 WEEKS ÷ A/R TURNOVER RATIO
= # DAYS TO COLLECT A/R**

numbers for you. You just need to make sure to look at them. With A/R Turnover Ratio, you can calculate how fast the A/R is being paid by dividing 52 weeks by it.

So if the average practice A/R is being paid in less than 30 days, it's doing really well. But if the A/R is being paid in more than 90 days, the practice is having issues turning A/R into cash, and that needs to be addressed. Now chances are good that the practice manager already has an **aging A/R** spreadsheet set up, which makes the process easier for you.

You need to keep an eye on the A/R. If you notice that a significant portion of the A/R is more than 90 days, it could mean issues with collection, but it may also mean that bad debt hasn't been written off and remains on the books. **Bad debt** is anything that you don't realistically expect to be able to collect. This eventually gets written off as an expense to clear it off of the books, and it lowers the income. Every business normally writes off some bad debt. Benchmarking against other practices may also help determine if there is an issue. You need to understand that deviance from the norm may be due to the type of patients or clients the practice sees.

**CASH RETURN ON SALES RATIO** tells you how well the practice is generating cash from practice charges. This only looks at cash and does not include A/R, but does help evaluate how well the practice is converting A/R to cash.

> How much cash does the company make
> from seeing patients/clients?
>
> **NET CASH from OPERATING ACTIVITIES ÷ NET SALES =**
> **CASH RETURN ON SALES**

You want a high ratio. If you are close to 1, you have a cash-only practice. If you have a significantly high amount of A/R that never gets converted to cash, the number will be much lower, and the practice may have cash flow issues.

## TAKEAWAYS

- The balance sheet shows how highly the practice or company is leveraged and how many assets are available to pay debts back if it goes belly up.
- The income statement shows how well the product and service lines are producing revenue and how the business is controlling its expenses.
- The cash flow statement shows how much cash is on hand to pay the firm's bills, dividends, or distributions.
- Accounts Receivable Turnover and the number of days to turnover will tell you how long it takes to collect cash from the A/R. The fewer the number of days the better.
- Cash return on sales shows how well the practice generates cash from sales or revenue.

**TO-DO LIST**

☐ Have your practice manager determine the A/R turnover rate, the number of days it takes to collect on A/R, and the cash return on sales.

☐ Compare the A/R numbers with previous time periods and the benchmark.

# PART IV

## PRACTICE FRAUD

Most practice owners I have met say they are concerned about losing money to office fraud and embezzlement, but very few really think it could ever happen to them. They look around the office and say, "Not my employees." I think physicians and professionals are a very trusting bunch. Unfortunately, the statistics tell a different story. According to a 2010 study by the Association of Certified Fraud Examiners, medical practices lose $25 billion annually, with an average loss at a practice of $160,000 with an average of 18 months that the embezzlement scheme goes undetected. A 2010 study by the Medical Group Management Association found that 83% of respondents had been affiliated with a medical practice that had encountered employee theft or embezzlement. The majority of the perpetrators will be long-time, trusted employees. Part IV will cover what motivates people to commit fraud, how they go about committing it, and what you should do about it.

# CHAPTER 16

# FRAUD BASICS

How and why do people commit fraud? This chapter will deal with the motivation to commit fraud and ways that employees might commit it. We will cover the following so you have an idea of what to look out for:

- How and Why People Commit Fraud
- Fraud Schemes

## HOW AND WHY PEOPLE COMMIT FRAUD

Most employees do not start out with the express purpose of committing fraud. It may start out of desperation. Some people may be living above their means, have a change in their living situation, be unhappy at work, or possibly notice lax controls and be tempted to try something. Many start small, not even intending to steal. They may "borrow" from the petty cash fund to pay a bill until their paycheck comes. But when they realize no one notices because there are few controls and little oversight, they fail to pay back the "loan" and may try it again.

Whether you are in a solo practice or a multispecialty group, you need to care about how the office runs. If you do not care, your staff will pick up on this and may begin rationalizing that it's okay to steal because you don't seem to care. When staff notices that you are not providing oversight, they can realize that there is an opportunity for embezzlement.

Practice owners also frequently turn over the oversight to the practice managers, thinking that managers know more about running the practice, and they rationalize that they, the professionals, don't have time to deal with oversight. By turning the practice oversight over to the practice manager and providing none yourself, you are giving the practice manager what he or she needs to embezzle. The people who are found guilty of fraud and embezzlement are most often those who are trusted, longtime employees, people who have deep ties with the owners and/or the owners' families.

In order to commit fraud, people need three things. They must have a need or incentive to steal, such as increasing personal debt, a child or a sick parent they need to provide for, living above their means, a divorce. They also need to have a reason or rationalization to steal, such as being a disgruntled employee, or a belief that the practice makes too much money and won't miss any that is taken. And lastly, they need to perceive an opportunity to steal.

The best tonic for embezzlement is to not let it happen in the first place. And the easiest way to do that is to show the staff that there is oversight and that you do care what happens in your practice. You would be surprised at how many professionals don't want to be burdened by providing that oversight. They want to delegate that responsibility. It's partly that they feel too busy taking care of patients and clients, but I also think it's because many aren't sure how to provide the oversight and what to look for. If you are in a larger physician or professional group, you could set up a management team made up of a few of the owners in your practice that changes every year to provide the necessary oversight. That way everyone shares in the pain.

## FRAUD SCHEMES

Once employees decide to embezzle, how do they do it? There are many possible schemes that they can use. By being aware of how it can occur, you can watch out for the schemes. If you separate duties between employees, they are less likely to gain the access to steal. When one person gets control of multiple processes, that individual gets the ability to cover his or her tracks. The schemes can be broken down into the following categories: credit card fraud, payroll fraud, petty cash and cash payment fraud, check fraud, accounts payable fraud, accounts receivable fraud, and supply theft fraud.

## CREDIT CARD FRAUD

Credit card fraud is fairly straightforward. Employees charge personal items to the company credit card and fail to provide receipts to verify that the purchases on the card were indeed for company business. For example, buying themselves lunch or office supplies for home use. Employees can also open up credit card mail solicitations and take out a "company" card in their own names or steal an owner's identity and open a card under the professional's name. Then they purchase personal items on the card and the office pays for it. How do you prevent this?

The first is to require that all purchases on the company card have receipts to verify the validity of the purchases. Next, the credit card statements should go directly to the owner, and he or she should be the only one to open it. If the statements go to the person paying the bills, they can be tampered with before the statements go to the practice owner. Once a month, the credit card statement should be reconciled with the receipts to make sure all charges are legitimate business expenses. If you are a solo practitioner, commingling personal finances with business finances is a terrible idea. For one, the IRS could come after you if you pay your personal expenses on the credit card bill with company money. And two, if you commingle your money, it will be easier for an employee to slip in personal charges that would have otherwise looked out of place on the statements.

The second protection is to authorize only one or two people to use the credit card. If there are fraudulent activities noted, it narrows down who could be committing them. The authorized credit card user should not be the person who has authority to pay the bills. If the authorized user and the person paying the bills is the same person, he or she could charge items and pay the bill without anyone knowing.

To further protect your practice from having employees open a "company" card in their own names, shred any credit card solicitations. You can also call the three main credit-reporting agencies and have them remove the company name from credit card solicitation lists. Also, compare the bank statements to the credit card statements once a month to ensure that there is not another credit card outstanding that is being paid in addition to the official business card. You can also check the amount paid on the credit card with the amount that came out of the checking account to make sure that the numbers match exactly.

## PAYROLL FRAUD

This is also straightforward. This can include padding the payroll by adding additional work hours, adding fake employees, or by adding family members as employees. The practice owner should approve any new employee. Do not leave this up to your practice manager unless you are assured that the duties are so separated that the manager cannot be involved in fraud. Be aware that taxes can be inflated and taken out of a paycheck while the net check amount appears the same. Then the perpetrator turns around and pockets the extra taxes. It is also a common scheme, if there is no oversight, for employees to give themselves raises or bonuses. This can all occur if one employee is in charge of preparing the payroll and signing the checks. Whoever is signing the checks needs to look at what they are signing, including the gross and net amounts of the checks and who is receiving a check in order to ensure that nothing seems different. Once you have done this several times, you will notice when something is not right.

Only the practice owners should sign the checks. And only one person should sign all of the payroll checks. When signing them, you must actually look at the checks to ensure that there are not extra fraudulent checks included. If there are multiple check signers, then an employee can have one owner sign a check and take an identical check to another to sign. Neither owner would know that the other had signed the exact same check.

Also, avoid hiring employees' family members or friends, if possible. Employee family members and friends have a greater incentive and ability to collude and commit fraud. And if the manager or bookkeeper hires a friend or family member, it may be tempting to inflate that person's paycheck. Your practice should have a policy of not hiring family members or friends of anyone who works at your practice, including the owners.

You should regularly compare the current payroll amount with previous payroll amounts and be aware of any new hires or firings. The payroll amounts should be close; if they're not, something untoward may be going on.

## PETTY CASH AND CASH PAYMENT FRAUD

Petty cash is what a business will hold in a cash box to cover change for patients or clients paying in cash or to pay for small expenses like postage. This is an area that is extremely at risk for stealing. Some practices find it a pain to have to replace the petty cash amount often and tend to hold a larger sum in the petty cash box. However, the larger the sum, the easier it is to steal. This is because the less often it is replenished and checked against a log, the less likely it is that a very small amount would be missed. So a business should limit the cash to less than $500. But the lower the better, such as $100. Also, the cash box needs to be locked on nights and weekends, and the person with the key should not have access to the cash box or be allowed to fill out receipts. Without these safeguards, it is very easy for someone to take money when no one is looking. The key needs to be kept securely away from the cash box or in a place that none of the employees know. It seems intuitive to keep the cash box secure, but you'd be surprised at how many unsecure cash boxes there are. A ledger with the receipts and the name of the employee who used the money also needs to be kept with the petty cash and reconciled every time the cash is replenished.

Patient or client cash payments are an easy target for embezzlement. When an employee has the ability to both collect the payment and enter it into the billing system, you have an open invitation to fraud, because a person can pocket the money and write off the payment in the system with no one knowing. The same is true if one person is allowed to collect the cash payment and deposit the money in the bank. The person can pocket the money and pretend the patient never showed for the appointment. The same is true if a single person makes out the deposit slip and deposits the money. It is easy enough not to list the cash payment on the deposit slip. Duties should be separated so that the person who collects the cash and makes out the deposit slip must turn it over to a different employee who verifies that the cash payments match the patients or clients seen for the day and then deposits the money. If this is done, it is much harder for one of them to hide the money unless they collude with each other.

One further note about cash payments—every cash payment should be recorded on a triplicate, pre-numbered receipt pad. And every patient or client should receive a printout of the payments for the visit before leaving the practice. A copy of the printout should also be retained to match against the list of patients or clients that were to be seen that day. That copy then goes to billing with a copy of the receipt so the billing staff can enter it into the computer. Co-pays, cash payments, and credit card payments need to be closed out at the end of the day and verified with the "those seen today" list. If you do not close out each day, it makes it harder to confirm that you have all of the credit card and cash receipts and allows more chance for fraud.

If patients or clients come in complaining about their bills always being wrong, it should raise red flags. If you also notice a lot of "special" discounts to patients or clients, or large amounts of write-offs, those too should raise red flags. It is easy for an employee to collect a payment and then "write off" the amount. The practice owner should be the only one to approve discounts and write-offs, and every month you need to see a printout of the patients or clients seen and the discounts given. Also, every day, you should get a printout of patients you have seen to compare with the list of people that were scheduled to be seen. This will keep patients or clients from disappearing off of the "seen list," which can prevent someone from pocketing the cash payment.

## CHECK FRAUD

You should never, as an owner, sign a blank check and hand it over to an employee. The same goes for the extra blank checks; they need to be locked up and not be available to the employees. If they are lying out in the open, anyone can take one and forge your name. Even better are the signature stamps. Again, you are asking for fraud, whether it's fraudulently stamping your signature to checks or even fraudulently writing prescriptions. You are responsible legally and financially for everything that happens, regardless of whether someone had criminal intent. If you have a signature stamp, destroy it. It is an easy way to commit malpractice—by having your staff stamp your name to documents or prescriptions without reviewing them.

Also, over a certain dollar amount, it may make sense to require two owners to sign a check. This is to make sure no one is forging a signature.

Bank statements, like credit card statements, should always be mailed directly to the practice owner or to the accountant, but never to the bookkeeper or any other person responsible for paying bills. The same goes for tax statements. There are numerous tales of managers stealing the taxes instead of paying them and then intercepting the statements so the owner never sees them. The IRS does not care if you didn't know that your taxes weren't being paid. When you get the bank statements, you need to make sure you know the vendors listed and to look at the canceled checks to make sure they are in order. Then review the front and the back of the checks to make sure no one forged the signatures or deposited one into their own account. If the same person who is writing the checks opens the statements, they can alter the statements or remove pages of canceled checks.

## ACCOUNTS PAYABLE FRAUD

Accounts payable consists of anything purchased on credit, including all of the invoices and bills for supplies, utilities, and so on. You need to make sure that only a practice owner can approve a new vendor. And that vendor needs to be checked out before accepting it in order to make sure it is a legitimate business that has appropriate products or services for your practice. There have been tales of managers and bookkeepers opening fake businesses and then issuing checks from the practice to the new fake vendor.

Beware of multiple invoices. Because of timing issues, it is not uncommon for a vendor to send out an initial invoice that gets paid. But while the check is in transit, the vendor sends out a second invoice before it receives your payment. You need to compare the bank statements with the receipts of paid bills to ensure that the bill was not paid twice. It is a common scheme for a manager or bookkeeper to pay a bill twice. He or she then turns around and requests a refund from the company and pockets that refund. The original bill should be marked paid with the invoice number. If a vendor insists on always dealing with the same employee, red flags should go up. The vendor employee and your employee may be colluding to bill for extras and split the profit between them.

In order to limit the chance of A/P fraud, the person approving the vendors and doing the ordering needs to be different than the person paying the bills. And every month the unopened bank statements need to be given to the owner, who should reconcile them with bill receipts.

## ACCOUNTS RECEIVABLE FRAUD

Anything that produces revenue for the practice that has not yet been paid for, like insurance claims and patient or client bills that are outstanding, are considered accounts receivable. Fraud can occur when an employee opens the mail and steals the check instead of giving it for deposit. Another fraudulent act is posting refunds to the patient or client account while not actually giving it to them and instead pocketing the refund.

The money needs to be separated from the person who enters the payment into the system and separate from the person who makes the deposit. The person who opens the mail should count the deposits and mark the checks "for deposit only." Someone else then enters the check into the A/R system. You never should allow the employees to cash checks.

## SUPPLY THEFT FRAUD

Supply theft is probably the most utilized fraud. Stolen office supplies, like paper, pens, and printer ink cartridges, are some of the most common things stolen. This also goes for DME, office and medical supplies, and drugs. All supplies need to be locked up and inventoried periodically. There should be limited access to these items and employees should not assume that because they work there the supplies are free. The price tags are small, but can add up to a significant loss of revenue.

### TAKEAWAYS

- Employees must have a need, a rationalization, and an opportunity in order to steal.
- Employees who are given too much access to processes have the ability to commit fraud. Separation of duties is a must. This includes the practice manager's duties as well.

**TO-DO LIST**

☐ Separate employees' duties so no one has complete autonomy over any of the systems.

☐ Make sure that you open the bank statements and reconcile them with the credit card statements.

☐ Approve all vendors.

☐ Keep the petty cash box, checks, and supplies locked up.

☐ Reestablish your practice's culture to one of expected oversight.

# CHAPTER 17

# RED FLAGS AND PREVENTION

N ow that you know the weak areas of a business that can be exploited, how do you realize if there is fraud going on? We will look at the red flags to be on the lookout for and how to take steps to prevent fraud from happening. This chapter will discuss the following:

- Red Flags
- Lack of Physician Oversight
- Fraud Prevention

## RED FLAGS

There are several red flags of which you should be aware. The first is if employees refuse to take vacation. These are also the people who work late or come in on the weekends to "catch up" on work. You think that they are hardworking employees, choosing to work overtime for the good of the practice, but these are the usual suspects for embezzlement. "What?" you say. "But they're such dedicated employees." While they are "hard at work" late at night or on weekends, they have plenty of time and lack of supervision to be able to cover their tracks. I'm not saying this happens every time, but if you have an employee who consistently works late or comes in on the weekends, you need to be aware of the possibility for embezzlement. This is especially true when the employee refuses to take vacation. They may fear that they will lose their control while they are away and will be at risk for being caught when someone else is performing their duties.

Be aware, too, of employees who volunteer for extra duties. This is especially true if they are amassing duties that put them in control of both the cash and the books. If you notice a practice or office manager who is now performing tasks that the front desk would usually do, you should have some concern. The same is also true if an employee is becoming more possessive of his or her duties and becoming more defensive, especially if you take away a duty or add an additional employee in his or her duty territory. Most employees would rather do less, not more. Be wary of those who want more work.

Lastly, be aware of the potential for employees to embezzle if they have a change in life circumstances, like a divorce or a sick child or parent, or if they're suddenly living beyond their means; buying new cars, bigger homes, or boats; developing anger toward the practice; or developing addictive habits like drug use or gambling. They now have a motivation to steal. Or they may already be stealing. Be on the lookout.

## LACK OF PROFESSIONAL OVERSIGHT

You may read this and say, "I don't have time to look at all of these items." Or "My practice manager can take care of this." Even your practice manager needs oversight. You must set the tone for your practice or you might as well leave signed blank checks lying around. If you provide no oversight, the prospect for fraud will be high. And don't think for a moment "fraud couldn't happen to me." It only doesn't happen if you take steps to prevent it.

The first time you try to tackle review of all of the ledgers, it might take you some time. But once you are used to looking at them, it should not take long to review them. If there are several partners, consider giving each one a responsibility so that each task may take each partner only 15 minutes.

Included in practice oversight is controlling computer access. I know countless professionals who hate computers and could care less about how their management system works. They allow their practice manager to set up the systems and create the passwords. If their practice manager was fired tomorrow and refused to give the passwords to unlock the system, they would be unable to access anything in the billing system. By allowing the practice manager to proceed in such a way, the owners are at the practice manager's mercy. Practice owners need to be in charge of the passwords and understand how the system runs. Never allow the practice manager or any other employee to have administrator access, or they can lock you out of your own system. There have been reports that the only thing a practice could do was to start over by buying a new system. In the same vein, all files should be backed up *off-site*, so that there is a copy that no employee can tamper with and a copy to have as backup in case you lose access to your system.

## FRAUD PREVENTION

The first thing is to create a culture in which the employees know that you are in charge and watching them. This will deter most people. They are less likely to try to steal if they know they are likely to get caught. There should be an employee handbook that clearly states that there are consequences for theft and fraud. And it should be mandatory that employees take vacations. The employees need to sign a statement stating that they received the handbook and have reviewed it.

The second is to do background checks on all employees. This includes education, employment, and even credit checks to be aware if someone has large outstanding debts. If you fail to do background checks on employees and they steal patient or client identities or harass employees or clients, you will be held legally liable. Although you cannot discriminate in hiring based simply on a background check, you can be held legally liable for *not* doing a background check.

Employees, especially those in charge of money, should be **bonded**. This is an insurance policy that covers a practice from losses sustained through employee misconduct like theft or embezzlement. There are several different types, so you will need to check with your insurance provider. The insurance may not pay for all of the money embezzled, but it may keep you from having to civilly prosecute the person in order to recoup the money.

The next thing is separation of duties with cross-training. If employees are getting rotated into different job duties, it is less likely that any stealing will occur. If it does occur, it is usually caught earlier. Employees will be less likely to steal if they know someone will be rotating into that duty and will discover what they are up to. And remember, the collecting, recording, and depositing of money should all be separated from each other.

Most importantly, practice owners need to be involved in reviewing un-opened bank and credit card statements and reconciling them each month with each other. Make sure the checks are legitimate and not forged or deposited to non-practice accounts. Owners should check out and approve each new vendor added to accounts payable and each employee added to payroll. Checks and supplies need to be locked up. This may seem oner-ous especially with clinical responsibilities. But if you split the tasks with other partners or have a rotating partner "management committee," it will be less onerous. This is your practice; you need to be in charge.

And lastly, keep your employees happy. If they are happy and feel that they are part of the team and not just another cog in the wheel, they are much less likely to be disgruntled, and they will be more likely to report people who are doing things they shouldn't be doing. Provide education for them on ethics and fraud prevention and how to spot fraud. Provide a way for employees to anonymously tell the partners about suspicions of fraud or stealing. This can be a locked box to which only the owner has a key.

## TAKEAWAYS

- The red flags of fraud include employees who refuse to take vaca-tion or who work late consistently, who volunteer for extra duties and become disgruntled when people rotate into their duties, or those who have a change in their life situation or are suddenly living beyond their means. Remember, most employees want less responsibility rather than more.
- Fraud prevention starts in the company culture. There must be an atmosphere of oversight and a way for employees to alert you if they see something suspicious.
- Employees with access to money should be bonded, and all employ-ees must have background checks. The practice is responsible if something happens.
- Separation and rotation of duties helps to prevent the ability to commit fraud.

**TO-DO LIST**

☐ Make sure employee duties are separated and that there is cross-training.

☐ Provide oversight of all employees, including the practice manager.

# CHAPTER 18

# WHAT TO DO IF YOU ARE A VICTIM OF FRAUD

You start noticing some of the red flags of fraud at your office. You begin to poke around and realize that you are indeed the victim of fraud. What do you do now? This chapter will look at the steps to take and what to consider when you are dealing with a case of fraud. We will look at the following topics:

- Collect Documents and Proof
- Notify the Insurance Company
- Fraud Investigator
- Prosecute, Fire, or Nothing?

## COLLECT DOCUMENTS AND PROOF

The first thing you need to do when you suspect fraud is to gather the proof that the fraud occurred and make copies. This should be done in complete secrecy. If you do not make copies and the perpetrator realizes that you are onto him or her, the person can destroy the documents and cover his or her tracks. If the person destroys the documents and the proof, there is nothing you can do, and no prosecution can take place.

## NOTIFY THE INSURANCE COMPANY

Once you have discovered the fraud, you need to notify your insurance company immediately if you have an employee misconduct policy. There is usually only a small window of opportunity that you have to notify them, and it usually begins when you first notice the issue. If you wait until you have all of the proof, you may nullify your insurance policy.

## FRAUD INVESTIGATOR

Consider hiring a fraud investigator if you suspect a very large sum of money has been embezzled. Until you have collected all of the documents and have proof of fraud in a secured location, you want to make sure that you don't alert the perpetrator to the presence of the fraud investigator. If it appears to be a large crime, you must be careful how the evidence is handled to avoid "evidence tampering." If the evidence is not collected and handled in the appropriate manner, it may be invalid in court.

## PROSECUTE, FIRE, OR NOTHING?

And finally, what should you do about the fraud? Do you prosecute? Do you fire the employee? Or do you do nothing? This depends on your circumstances, the value of the employee, and the amount stolen. It is very common for the amount lost during fraudulent schemes to be more than what you can determine and prove on the surface and becomes significantly larger with an investigation.

As far as pursuing prosecution, you have two choices. The first is a **civil lawsuit,** which tends to be expensive and drawn out. This will be at your own expense and does not end with a criminal record if the person is found guilty. Even if you are awarded damages, the perpetrator may not be able to pay up.

Your other option is a **criminal prosecution**. If this is the angle you decide to take, the state pays for the prosecution and the embezzler will end up with a criminal record if found guilty. If the person does not end up with a criminal record, they may have a much easier time of taking advantage of the next employer. Because of the fear of a slander lawsuit, most previous employers will only state that the employee worked for them if asked by a potential new employer about the person. They usually will not state that they were involved in fraud. However, if the person has a criminal conviction, that will follow them on every job application. In many cases involving criminal prosecution, the prosecutor will also ask for reimbursement of the damages to the practice.

You may also choose just to let the employee go instead of advertising to your other employees and the public that you have an embezzlement issue if you are concerned about the practice's image. Whatever your choice, do not feel guilty about going after the employee, even if they have been a trusted employee for 20 years. Regardless of the actions taken, you first need to secure the evidence. Then you can decide how you would like to proceed.

This is critical: Make sure you have undeniable proof before you accuse an employee of fraud. If you don't have the proof, you might just find yourself on the other side of a slander lawsuit. Check with your attorney about what you are allowed to say regarding an ex-employee to protect yourself from slander if someone calls you for a previous employment reference check.

## TAKEAWAYS

- There is usually only a small window of opportunity to notify the insurance company of fraud.
- Evidence needs to be secured before any action is taken on suspected fraud.
- Make sure not to alert the perpetrator before all evidence is secured off-site.
- Your options for fraud prosecution are civil litigation, criminal prosecution, or nothing.

## TO-DO LIST

- ☐ If fraud happens, notify the insurance company immediately.
- ☐ Secure all evidence off-site and avoid alerting the perpetrator.

# CONCLUSION

Hopefully by now you have picked up the basics of financial management. It is important to get the boring, mundane items like budgeting and learning how to read a financial statement out of the way. Do not blow these items off. Use this book as a reference, as needed. If your financial advisor is talking about a whole life policy or investing you into options, go re-read that section. Do your homework so that you can have an intelligent conversation with your advisor and truly be able to decide what is in your best interest.

Remember that handling your finances is not hard, but it does require discipline and perseverance. Your manager or bookkeeper can prepare many of the items covered in the financial statement section. But you need to make sure that you look closely at the numbers on the statements that they produce for you. Force yourself to take the next few weeks to sit down and do the things that you find hard. Make a budget, read your financial statements, review the financial ratios, or look at your 401k offerings. Once you have forced yourself to do it once, it becomes easier the next time. And eventually it becomes second nature, and you will wonder why you ever shied away from managing your money yourself. Remember, this is neither rocket science nor neurosurgery. You can do this. Now go pass on your knowledge to everyone around you.